SCOTS-IRISH LINKS
1575-1725

PART TEN

by
David Dobson

CLEARFIELD

Copyright © 2017
by David Dobson
All Rights Reserved

Printed for Clearfield Company by
Genealogical Publishing Company
Baltimore, Maryland
2017

ISBN 978-0-8063-5833-8

Made in the United States of America

INTRODUCTION

The Plantation of Ulster by Scots in the seventeenth century is a well-known established fact. Family historians, however, require very specific reference material, which is generally missing from the published accounts of the migration and settlement of thousands of Scots in Ireland at that time. While the majority of settlers were from the Scottish Lowlands, some, especially in the late sixteenth century, were Highlanders. It should also be noted that the Presbyterians were in the majority, but there was a sizable minority that were Episcopalians and a few that were Roman Catholics. Also, though the main area of settlement was in Ulster, it is evident that a number settled further south.

Part ten of *Scots-Irish Links, 1575-1725* attempts to identify more of these Scottish settlers and their children. It is based largely on research carried out into both manuscript and published sources located in Scotland, Ireland, England, and the Netherlands. It should be noted that the index of names found in wills and other deeds do include a few people of Anglo-Irish or indigenous Irish origin.

Within a few generations, the descendants of these Ulster Scots emigrated in substantial numbers across the Atlantic, where, as the Scotch-Irish, they made a major contribution to the settlement and development of colonial America.

David Dobson, Dundee, Scotland, 2017

REFERENCES

ActsPCCol	=	Acts of the Privy Council, Colonial
APCE	=	Acts, Privy Council, England
ATS	=	Accounts of the Treasurer of Scotland
BL	=	British Library, London
BMF	=	Belfast Merchant Families
C	=	A Census of Ireland circa 1659
CalSPDom	=	Calendar, State Papers, Domestic

Carew	=	Carew Manuscripts, London
CLRO	=	City of London Record Office
CPRI	=	Calendar of Patent Rolls, Ireland
CSPI	=	Calendar of State Papers, Ireland
CTP	=	Calendar of Treasury Papers, series
DRD	=	Dublin Register of Deeds
ECA	=	Edinburgh City Archives
F	=	Fasti Ecclesiae Scoticanae
FIB	=	Flemish Influence in Britain, Glasgow, 1930
GAA	=	Amsterdam Archives
GAR	=	Rotterdam Archives

GBR	=	Glasgow Burgess Roll
HM	=	Hamilton Manuscripts
HMC	=	Historical Manuscript Commission, London
IC	=	Ireland under the Commonwealth, Manchester, 1913
LC	=	Calendar of the Laing Charters, Edinburgh, 1899
MM	=	Montgomery Manuscripts
NRAS	=	National Register Archives, Scotland
NRS	=	National Records of Scotland

157

PCC	=	Prerogative Court of Canterbury
PRONI	=	Public Record Office, Northern Ireland
REB	=	Edinburgh Burgess Roll
RPCS	=	Register of the Privy Council of Scotland
SM	=	Scots Magazine, series
SP	=	The Scots Peerage
TBB	=	The Belfast Book
TCD	=	Trinity College, Dublin
TNA	=	The National Archives, London
UJA	=	Ulster Journal of Archaeology
UPB	=	Ulster Port Books

ABERCROMBY, ADAM, of Killerty, County Down, aged 73, petitioned King Charles I on behalf of himself and of Margaret Julius, sister and heir to Alexander Julius late of Leith in Scotland, 1633. [CSPI]

ABERCROMBIE, JAMES, a merchant aboard the Elizabeth of Belfast in 1690. [NRS.E72.12.16]

ABERCROMBIE, JAMES, son of the Duke of Hamilton, at Limerick, 7 February 1700. [NRS.GD406.1.4735]

ABERCROMBY, THOMAS, was granted patent of denization on 5 July 1631. [CPRI]

ABERCROMBY, THOMAS, obtained land in County Leitrim from James Creighton, 30 November 1631. [CPRI]

ACHESON, Sir ARCHIBALD, was appointed Master of Chancery on 23 November 1625. [CPRI]

ACHESON, WILLIAM, was robbed of his sword by Neal Boy Milnattalie of Clady, County Armagh, in 1622. [CPRI]

ADAIR, ANNA, relict of Thomas Kennedy sometime minister of the Gospel in Newton in the Kingdom of Ireland, testament, 1719, Comm. Glasgow. [NRS]

ADAIR, ARCHIBALD, Dean of Raphoe, County Donegal, sasines, Wigton, 19 June 1618. [NRS.RS1.389/390]; was appointed Bishop of Killally and Achonry, in the province of Connaught in 1629. [CPRI]

ADAIR, Sir ROBERT, of Balmenock in Ireland, was granted the lands of Drummor in Scotland on 15 July 1698. [NRS.RGS.75.14]

ADAIR, Sir ROBERT, a petition, 1705. [TNA.SP44.241/198]

ADARE, WILLIAM, late of Ballymannagh, County Antrim, and his son and heir Robert Adare, 2 December 1628. [CPRI]

ADAIR, WILLIAM, in Belfast, 1669. [PRONI.T307A]

ADAIR, WILLIAM, master of the Prosperity of Belfast in 1689. [NRS.E72.19.15]

ADAIR, WILLIAM, born 1650, died in February 1698. [Antrim gravestone]

AGNEW, ALEXANDER, of Belymaglach, died 29 August 1700, husband of Jane McQuoid, born 1652, died 7 December 1723. [Comber gravestone, County Down]

AGNEW, DAVID, a merchant aboard the James of Belfast at Barbados in 1668. [Acts PCCol.755/1041]

AGNEW, GEORGE, in Belfast in 1669. [PRONI.T307A]

AGNEW, JAMES, born 1685, died 10 May 1727. [Dromara Cathedral gravestone]

AGNEW, JOHN, in Belfast in 1669. [PRONI.T307A]

AGNEW, PATRICK, in Belfast in 1669. [PRONI.T307A]

AGNEW, PATRICK, in Kilwaughter, will, 1725. [PRONI.T700.1]

AGNEW, THOMAS, in Belfast, a book, 1686. [NRS.GD154.935]

AHAGARTIE, JAMES, a leech from Ireland, 1579. [ATS.XIII.262]

AIKENHEAD, PATRICK, born 1713, a book-keeper from Dublin, an indentured servant bound from London to Jamaica in 1731. [CLRO]

ALEXANDER, JAMES, late of the Irish Treasury in Dublin, petitioned the Privy Council of Scotland, 1691. [RPCS.xvi.654]

ALEXANDER, JOHN, a gentleman in Dublin, was admitted as a burgess and guilds-brother of Glasgow in 1718. [GBR]

ALEXANDER, or MCALEXANDER, FERGUS, tutor of Dalreoch, graduated MA from Glasgow University in 1635, minister at Kilmud in Ireland, admitted as minister of Barr, Ayrshire, in 1653 but dismissed by the Privy Council in 1662, returned in August 1687, died after 9 February 1688. He married Jean, daughter of William McKerrell of Hillhouse, she died in May 1691. [F.V.17]

ALEXANDER, JEROME, in St John Hoys Alley, Dublin, in 1659. [C]

ALEXANDER, THOMAS, a soldier of Colonel Bayley's Regiment, 22 February 1648. [HMC.Ormonde.ii.70]

ALEXANDER, Sir WILLIAM, of Menstrie in Scotland, purchased the Manor of Dacostrose and Portlagh also the watermill of Cargyn in County Donegal, from Sir James Cunningham of Glengarnoch in Scotland on 26 February 1628. On 14 January 1629 Sir William was granted 1000 acres in the Barony of O'Neilan, County Armagh. [CPRI]

ALGOE, ROBERT, a gentleman in Karrowkill, parish of Tully, Barony of Killmccrenan, County Donegal, 1659. [C]

ALLEN, HUGH, born 1656, died 1734, husband of Elizabeth Aresbal [Archibald?]. [Rasbee gravestone, County Antrim]

ALLERDICE, WILLIAM, from Aberdeen, took the Oath of Allegiance and Supremacy to King Charles II, on 18 February 1671 in Ireland.

ALLISON, HUGH, in Island Flacky, Liberty of Coleraine, 1720. [UJA.VII.10]

ANDERSON, AGNES, died 17 December 1680, wife of John Braynen, [1627-1705. [Comber gravestone, County Down]

ANDERSON, ANDREW, a tenant in Bangor town, County Down, 1681. [HM]

ANDERSON, GEORGE, a merchant in Belfast, 1689. [RPCS.XIII.583]

ANDERSON, HENRY, a Freeman of Belfast in 1640. [TBB]

ANDERSON, JOHN, a tenant in Bangor town, County Down, 1681. [HM]

ANDERSON, ROBERT, a tenant in Bangor town, County Down, 1681. [HM]

ANDERSON, WILLIAM, in town of Letterkenny, parish of Cornwall, Barony of Killmccrenan, County Donegal, 1659. [C]

ANDERSON, ..., a widow, a tenant in Bangor town, County Down, in 1681. [HM]

ANISTON, JAMES, a tenant in Ballywaltertown, County Down, 1681. [HM]

ARCHIBALD, JOHN, born 1653, died 3 August 1719, husband of Margaret Alland who died 28 October 1707. [Rasbee gravestone, County Antrim]

ARMOUR, JAMES, born 1601, a tanner in Bangor, died 20 June 1672. [Old Abbey Church gravestone, Bangor, County Down]

ARMSTRONG, ANDREW, in Mauristown, County Kildare, will refers to his wife in Linlithgow, West Lothian, his uncle

Archibald Armstrong, his brothers Hugh and Charles
Armstrong, his nephew Edmond Armstrong son to his brother
William Armstrong deceased, his brother-in-law Milo Bagot;
witnesses John Claxton a gentleman in Togginstown, County
Kildare, Thomas Pender a yeoman in Newbridge, County
Kildare, Patrick Carrell servant to Robert Parkinson in Dublin,
Thomas Mullock and James Wilde both gentlemen in Dublin,
probate 22 November 1723. [DRD]

ARMSTRONG, CHRISTOPHER, a gentleman in Garriduff,
barony of Tireagh, County Sligo, 1659. [C]

ARMSTRONG, JOHN, the elder, a soldier of Colonel
Bayley's Regiment, 22 February 1648. [HMC.Ormonde.ii.70]

ARMSTRONG, JOHN, the younger, a soldier of Colonel
Bayley's Regiment, 22 February 1648. [HMC.Ormonde.ii.70]

ARMSTRONG, JOHN, a gentleman in Coolumphill, parish of
Magherycoolemoney, County Fermanagh, 1659. [C]

ARMSTRONG, ROBERT, in the barony of Magheryboy,
County Fermanagh, 1631. [PRONI.T.934]

ARNOTT, GEORGE, a Captain of the Earl of Dunbarton's
Regiment which landed at Kinsale in April 1679, later in
Killeagh. [CPRI][HMC.Ormonde.ii.219]

ARNOTT, JAMES, in Gartondarragh, County Fermanagh,
1659. [C]

AUCHENLECK, ROBERT, rector of Killibeggs, County
Donegal, testament, 26 December 1689, Comm. Edinburgh.
[NRS]

AUCHMUTY, JOHN, in Newtown, County Longford, will
refers to his son Richard, Reverend Luke Stirling in Mount
Dutton, County Meath, Francis Featherston a gentleman in

Greenrock, County Longford; witnesses John Boyle a student at Trinity College in Dublin, William French clerk to Henry Buckley a Notary Public in Dublin, and said Henry Buckley, probate 13 August 1726. [DRD]

AULD, JAMES, a tenant in Bangor town, County Down, 1681. [HM]

BAILLY, ALEXANDER, a gentleman in Inchargy and Ballymullen, parish of Ballywalter, Barony of The Ards, County Down, in 1659. [C]

BAILY, ALEXANDER, a tenant in Ringdufferin, County Down, in 1681. [HM]

BAILLIE, DAVID, a Lieutenant of the Earl of Dunbarton's Regiment which landed at Kinsale in April 1679. [HMC.Ormonde.ii.219]

BAILLY, EDWARD, a gentleman in Ballygargen, parish of Ballywalter, Barony of The Ards, County Down, in 1659. [C]

BAILLIE, JAMES, of Inniscargie, County Down, a lease, 1687. [PRONI.D24]

BAILLY, JOHN, a gentleman in Inchargy and Ballymullen, parish of Ballywalter, Barony of The Ards, County Down, in 1659. [C]

BAILLY, JOHN, a tenant in Creviheavarick, Hollywood town, County Down, in 1681. [HM]

BAILY, JOHN, tenant of Ballygarven, County Down, in 1681. [HM]

BAILY, JOHN, tenant of Inishargie, Ballyorgie, and Kircurbin Mill, County Down, in 1681. [HM]

BAILY, ['Bely'], WILLIAM JOHN, from Ireland, married....
Annetie Negenduysent, from Scotland {!}, in Rotterdam, the
Netherlands, on 7 August 1695. [Scots Kirk register there]
[GAR]

BAIRD, HARRY, in Dublin, deeds, 1702.
[NRS.RD2.86.1.62/71/189/429; RD2.88.1.264]

BAIRD, JOHN, a soldier of Colonel Bayley's Regiment, 22
February 1648. [HMC.Ormonde.ii.70]

BAIRD, JOHN, a merchant in Dublin, a deed, 1702.
[NRS.RD2.86.1.264]

BAIRD, ROBERT, a gentleman in St Johnston, County
Donegal, will refers to his son Thomas Baird, his grandson
Charles McFarland, Archibald Woods in Transallagh, County
Donegal, Archibald Conyngham a gentleman in Londonderry,
William Cowan son of John Cowan, Patrick Bedlow in Church
Street, Strabane, Andrew Park in Castle Street, Strabane,
Alexander Jameson and Claud Scott in Strabane; witnesses
Alexander Park an innkeeper in Londonderry, John Harvey a
gentleman in Drumore County Donegal, James Cochrane
merchant in Londonderry, Alexander Richardson a gentleman
in Dublin, and David Wilson, probate, 21 June 1714. [DRD]

BALFOUR, BARTHOLEMEW, a gentleman in Lislost,
parish of Aghahurchur, County Fermanagh, 1659. [C]

BALFOUR, CHARLES, in Lisneskea, parish of Aghahurchur,
County Fermanagh, 1659. [C]

BALFOUR, DAVID, in Aghor Castle, County Tyrone, 26
December 1626. [CPRI]

BALFOUR, JAMES, a land grant on 21 July 1626. [CPRI]

BALFOUR, Lord JAMES, was granted land in the barony of

Knocknyny, County Fermanagh, also the manor of Carrowshee there, 26 August and 6 October 1629. [CPRI]; Baron of Clanawley, petitioned King Charles I that his lands would descend to his kinsman Sir William Balfour, 1635. [CSPI]

BALFOUR, Sir WILLIAM, in Lisneskea, parish of Aghahurchur, County Fermanagh, 1659. [C]

BALIE, JOHN, in County Tyrone, 17 July 1657, son of William Balie. [NRS.GD156.274]

BANNERMAN, GEORGE, a Lieutenant of the Earl of Dunbarton's Regiment which landed at Kinsale in April 1679. [HMC.Ormonde.ii.219]

BARCLAY, ANDREW, an Ensign of the Earl of Dunbarton's Regiment which landed at Kinsale in April 1679. [HMC.Ormonde.ii.219]

BARCLAY, GAVIN, Precentor of Cashel, 2 May 1629. [CPRI]

BARCLAY, HUGH, Rector of Dromore, was granted lands in the Barony of Omey, County Tyrone, 29 February 1631. [CPRI]

BARCLAY, HUGH, a gentleman in Lifford, parish of Lifford, Barony of Raphoe, County Donegal, 1659. [C]

BARKLEY, JAMES, of Belyselloch, born 1646, died 17 August 1710, father of James, a divinity student, born 1675, died 16 July 1693, Alexander, a counsellor at law, born 1677, died 28 October 1705, and Ann, born 1683, died 20 February 1705. [Old Abbey Church gravestone, Bangor, County Down]

BARCLAY, ROBERT, of Leiford, Ireland, 16…. [NRS.GD3.1.3.27]

BARCLAY, WILLIAM, a gentleman in Rafgill, parish of Bangor, Barony of the Ards, County Down, 1659. [C]

BARCLAY, WILLIAM, a gentleman in Ballow, parish of Bangor, Barony of the Ards, County Down, 1659. [C]

BARCLAY, WILLIAM, a Lieutenant of the Earl of Dunbarton's Regiment which landed at Kinsale in April 1679. [HMC.Ormonde.ii.219]

BARCLAY, WILLIAM, a tenant in Hollywood Town, County Down, in 1681. [HM]

BAYLEY, EDWARD, of Lisgan, was granted patent of denization on 5 July 1631. [CPRI]

BELL, ADAM, a Lieutenant of the Earl of Dunbarton's Regiment which landed at Kinsale in April 1679. [HMC.Ormonde.ii.219]

BELL, JAMES, of Bellystockert, born 1642, died 8 April 1715. [Comber gravestone, County Down]

BELL, JOHN, a soldier of Colonel Bayley's Regiment, 22 February 1648. [HMC.Ormonde.ii.69]

BELL, JOHN, of Balykigle, born 1619, died 27 December 1701, husband of Barbara Dickson, born 1614, died 18 May 1686. [Comber gravestone, County Down]

BELL, JOHN, of New Comber, born 1648, died 1 April 1721. [Comber gravestone, County Down]

BELL, JOHN, a gentleman in Aughnacreevy, County Cavan, will refers to his son Andrew Bell, grandson John Bell, his brother Ralph Hines; witnesses Thomas Clarke in Corlismore, County Cavan, Elizabeth Monypenny in Woodtown, County

Meath, John Cunningham in Loughcrew, County Meath, and
James Cunningham in Dublin, probate 1 June 1727. [DRD]

BIGGER, JOHN, and MARGARET MCKIBBIN, were
married in Dundonald Presbyterian Church, County Down, in
November 1680. [Dundonald Kirk Session Register]

BIGHAM. JAMES, a tenant in Bangor town, County Down, in
1681. [HM]

BLACK, JOHN, from Ireland, married Plasant Parker from
England in the Reformed Church, Rotterdam, the Netherlands,
on 26 January 1642. [GAR]

BLACK, ..., late of Lurganbaneroe, died in August 1710.
[Dromore Cathedral gravestone]

BLACKWOOD, JAMES, born 1591, merchant and Provost of
Bangor, died 22 May 1663. [Old Abbey Church gravestone,
Bangor, County Down]

BLACKWOOD, JAMES, a tenant in Bangor town, County
Down, in 1681. [HM]

BLACKWOOD, JAMES, born 1695, died 25 December 1749,
husband of Isabel Whyte, born 1702, died 5 June 1720. [Old
Abbey Church gravestone, Bangor, County Down]

BLACKWOOD, JOHN, a tenant in Ballymacormick and
Ballyleely near Bangor, County Down, in 1681. [HM]; John
Blackwood of Ballyleidy, born 1662, died 11 July 1720,
husband of Ann Blackwood, born 1673, died 12 September
1741. [Old Abbey Church gravestone, Bangor, County Down]

BLACKWOOD, JOHN, a tenant in Island McKee, Manor of
Ballydeine, County Down, 1681. [HM]

BLACKWOOD, JOHN, born 1689, a merchant in Bangor, died 22 November 1759, husband of Agnes Phimiston, born 1707, died 5 August 1778. [Old Abbey Church gravestone, Bangor, County Down]

BLACKWOOD, WILLIAM, a merchant burgess of Edinburgh, appointed his wife Agnes Burdon as his factor during his absence in Ireland, 13 October 1662. [ECA.MB.II.bundle44/1891]

BLAIR, ALEXANDER, in Bolinhona, County Londonderry, 1659. [C]

BLAIR, JOHN, born 1673, died 27 October 1720, husband of Janet Linn, born 1675, died 20 January 1730, parents of Jane, Mary, and Catherine. [Ballywillin gravestone, County Antrim]

BLAIR, ROBERT, a gentleman in Derniecross townland, County Londonderry, 1659. [C]

BLAIR, SAMUEL, born 1667, died 20 March 1754. [Raloo gravestone, County Antrim]

BLAIR, WILLIAM, a gentleman in Lisnamuck townland, parish of Aughadowey, County Londonderry, 1659. [C]

BLAKELY, JOHN, jr., a tenant in Bangor town, County Down, 1681. [HM]

BLANE, THOMAS, a merchant in Dublin, versus Patrick Young a writer in Maybole, Ayrshire, 1695. [NRS.CS228B/1/3/2]; letters 1696-1701. [NRS.GD109.2230]; a merchant in Dublin, formerly in Enoch, deeds, 1702. [NRS.RD2.86.2.716/762]

BLEAKLY, JOHN, sr., a tenant in Bangor town, County Down, in 1681. [HM]

BOOWMAN, JOHN, born 1667, died 7 June 1728. [Comber gravestone, County Down]

BOYD, ANDREW, in Ballymcilluanan, born 1678, died 20 November 1734, husband of Jean ..., parents of Andrew. [Ballywillin gravestone, County Antrim]

BOYD, Colonel DAVID, in County Down, 1610. [LC.1582]

BOYD, DAVID, a tenant in Portavogie, The Ards, County Down, 1681. [HM]

BOYD, DAVID, a merchant in Dublin, was admitted as a burgess and guilds-brother of Glasgow on 24 July 1717. [GBR][NRS.GD26.8.84]

BOYD, HUGH, in Drumvillon, Barony of Carey, 1720. [UJA.VII.11]

BOYD, HUGH, in Drumnacross, Barony of Carey. 1720. [UJA.VII.11]

BOYD, JOHN, in the townlands of Drumnovodderry, County Down, 1659. [C]

BOYD, JOHN, in Telyhubert, born 1640, died 27 December 1707.

BOYD JOHN, a gentleman in Rathmore, will refers to his wife, his children James, Elizabeth and Jane, son in law John McDowell, James Crawford, John McDowell, Alexander Adair; witnesses Alexander Brown in Moyedom, Josias Ennis a yeoman in Rathbeg, James Craig a linen draper in Ballynoe, all in County Antrim, probate 11 August 1721. [DRD]

BOYD, Lady MARY, widow of Thomas Boyd, of the city of Dublin, a bond, dated at Kilmarnock, Ayrshire, in 1727. [NRS.GD3991]

BOYD, MATTHEW, a gentleman in Monaghan in 1659. [C]

BOYD, ROBERT, son and heir of Colonel David Boyd deceased, inherited land in Ulster purchased by his father, 20 July 1626. [CPRI]

BOYD, ROBERT, supercargo aboard the Northsbore of Londonderry bound for Portugal, arrested and imprisoned in Southampton charged with trading with France in 1705. [TNA.SP42.120.61; SP44.105.120]

BOYD, THOMAS, a gentleman in Portevoggy, parish of Balleharbert, barony of The Ards, County Down, in 1659. [C]

BOYD, THOMAS, a merchant in Dublin, imprisoned 22 May 1663. [CSPI]

BOYD, WILLIAM, minister of Macosquin, County Londonderry, emigrated to New England in 1718.

BRADLEY, THOMAS, a tenant in Ballynegarrick, Hollywood town, County Down, in 1681. [HM]

BRADLEY, THOMAS, a tenant in Bangor town, County Down, 1681. [HM]

BRICE, ARCHIBALD, 1 November1614, testament of John Lockhart of Barr, Comm. Glasgow. [NRS]

BRICE, ARCHIBALD, sometime a merchant in Dublin, afterwards in Glasgow, testament, 1 August 1691 Comm Glasgow. [NRS]

BRICE, CHRISTOPHER, was granted 1189 acres in County West Meath and 466 acres in King's County, 1 May 1629. [CPRI]

BRICE, EDWARD, born 1563, minister in Templecorran from

1613 until his death in 1630, father of Robert Brice a merchant in Dublin. [Templecorran gravestone]

BRICE, EDWARD, a Presbyterian, a merchant and a burgess of Belfast from 1697 to 1707. [BMF]

BRICE, RANDAL, in Lisnagarvy, County Antrim, will, 1697. [PRONI.T700.1]

BRUCE, Lieutenant ROBERT, in Killoyne parish, Coleraine, 1659. [C]

BRICE, ROBERT, of Cranagh, County Down, 1663. [PRONI.T307]

BRUCE, THOMAS, a gentleman in the parish of Taghboine, County Donegal, 1659. [C]

BROTHERSTON, ROBERT, in Carrickfergus, a letter, 1689. [NRS.GD406.1.3527]

BROWN, GEORGE, a tenant in Cullintragh, County Down, 1681. [HM]

BROWN, ROBERT, formerly of Gabrochill, Stewarton parish, Ayrshire, thereafter in Ireland, a deed, 1623. [NRAS.3957.7]

BROWN, WILLIAM, a tenant in Bangor town, County Down, 1681. [HM]

BROWN, ..., a widow, a tenant in Ballywaltertown, County Down, 1681. [HM]

BROWN, ..., the widow, tenant in the Church Quarter of Dundonell, County Down, in 1681. [HM]

BRUCE, ROBERT, in Killead, will, 1728. [PRONI.T700.1]

BUCHANAN, GEORGE, a gentleman in Cullachybeg, parish of Raphoe, barony of Raphoe, County Donegal, 1659. [C]

BUCHANAN, JAMES, a Captain of the Earl of Dunbarton's Regiment which landed at Kinsale in April 1679. [HMC.Ormonde.ii.219]

BUCHANAN, JOHN, a tenant in Fuly, married Joan Sampson, in 1694. [TCD.750.367]

BUCHANAN, WALTER, in town of Letterkenny, parish of Cornwall, barony of Killmccrenan, County Donegal, 1659. [C]

BUCHANAN, WILLIAM, was presented to the Deaneries of Killala and Achonry in the Diocese of Killala, 1 February 1629. [CPRI]

BUCHANAN, WILLIAM, a gentleman in Black Abbey, parish of Gray Abbey, Barony of The Ards, County Down, in 1659. [C]

BURNETT, JOHN, of Ballyleek, County Monaghan, was pardoned on 14 July 1631. [CPRI]

BURNSIDE, JOHN, a merchant in Silver Street, Londonderry, 1659. [C]

BUSBY, JOHN, born 1706, died 1716. [Comber gravestone, County Down]

BUTLE, DAVID, a Presbyterian, a merchant and a burgess of Belfast from 1700 to his death in1707. [BMF]

BYERS, GEORGE, a tenant in Ballywaltertown, County Down, 1681. [HM]

BYERS, WILLIAM, a tenant in Ballywaltertown, County Down, 1681. [HM]

BYRES, ..., a widow, a tenant in Ballywaltertown, County Down, in 1681. [HM]

CALDWELL, HARRY, a gentleman in Enniskillen, County Fermanagh, 1659. [C]

CALDWELL, THOMAS, petitioned King Charles I for a grant of 2000 acres in Ireland, 1634. [CSPI]

CALDWELL, WILLIAM, in Duncrum, Magilligan, County Londonderry, emigrated to New England in 1718. [PRONI.D673.4]

CALHOUNE, JAMES, in Corky, parish of Ray, Barony of Raphoe, County Donegal, 1659. [C]

CALHOUNE, JOHN, in town of Letterkenny, parish of Cornwall, Barony of Killmccrenan, County Donegal, 1659. [C]

CALHOUNE, PETER, in town of Letterkenny, parish of Cornwall, Barony of Killmccrenan, County Donegal, 1659. [C]

CALHOUNE, WALTER, in Leck, parish of Leck, Barony of Raphoe, County Donegal, 1659. [C]

CAMPBELL, AGNES, Lady Kintyre, spouse of Tarloch O'Neil Tirconnell in Ireland, a deed 1573. [NRS.GD1.506.5]

CAMPBELL, ALEXANDER, a Lieutenant of the Earl of Dunbarton's Regiment which landed at Kinsale in April 1679. [HMC.Ormonde.ii.219]

CAMPBELL, ANN, in Dublin, a will, 1729. [PRONI.T700.1]

CAMPBELL, CHARLES, a gentleman in parish of Newtown,

Barony of the Ards, County Down, 1659. [C]

CAMPBELL, CHARLES, in Donaghadee, Member of the
Irish Parliament for the borough of Newton Ards in 1661.
[MM]

CAMPBELL, CHARLES, in Dublin, letters, 1700.
[NRS.GD109.2627]; will, 1725. [PRONI.T700.1]

CAMPBELL, COLIN, a gentleman in Belliherin, parish of
Clandevadock, Barony of Killmccrenan, County Donegal,
1659. [C]

CAMPBELL, JAMES, a Lieutenant of the Earl of
Dunbarton's Regiment which landed at Kinsale in April 1679.
[HMC.Ormonde.ii.21]

CAMPBELL, JANET, in Ireland, daughter of David Campbell
in Dunevin, Ayrshire, mentioned in his testament dated 1639.
She was directed to keep her sister Marion Campbell with her
and to look after her. Testament confirmed Comm. Glasgow.
1643. [NRS]

CAMPBELL, Sir JOHN, a lieutenant in the service of King
James at the siege of Donavegge Castle, Ireland, 1614. [Carew
mss.vol.600, 6]

CAMPBELL, JOHN, a gentleman in the townlands of
Berecra, Donoghmore, County Down, 1659. [C]

CAMPBELL, JOHN, a gentleman in Belliherin, parish of
Clandevadock, Barony of Killmccrenan, County Donegal,
1659. [C]

CAMPBELL, JOHN, a tenant in Bangor town, County Down,
in 1681. [HM]

CAMPBELL, JOHN, in Lismureity, Barony of Carey. 1720. [UJA.VII.11]

CAMPBELL, JOSIAS, in Dublin, will refers to his mother Margaret Campbell, his wife Letitia, his children Samuel, George, Margaret, Agnes, Letitia, Catherine, Jane and Alice, Dr George Martin in Dublin, Patrick Orr a gentleman in Clough, County Antrim, Josias Cunningham and his son Daniel,; witnesses James Reilly Councillor at Law in Dublin, Thomas Richardson an attorney of the Court of King's Bench, James Anderson a gentleman in Dublin son of Francis Anderson an attorney of the Court of the Exchequer, Reverend James Teate of Crochan, County Cavan, and his wife Anna, Mary Mitchell schoolmistress of Crochan, John Ryan a gentleman in Dublin, and Francis Mahon a merchant in Dublin, probate 2 November 1722. [DRD]

CAMPBELL, PATRICK, a gentleman in Magherihober, parish of Clandevadock, Barony of Killmccrenan, County Donegal, 1659. [C]

CAMPBELL, PATRICK, a bookseller in Dublin, 1689. [RPCS.XIII.580]

CAMPBELL, ROBERT, a gentleman in Corin, parish of Clandevadock, Barony of Killmccrenan, County Donegal, 1659. [C]

CAMPBELL, ROBERT, a tenant in Ballywaltertown, County Down, 1681. [HM]

CAMPBELL, THOMAS, in Newton Limnavady, Londonderry, 1659. [C]

CARLYLE, LUDOVICK, petitioned King Charles I for a grant of 2000 acres in Ireland, 1634. [CSPI]

CARMICHAEL, JAMES, a tenant in Bangor town, County Down, in 1681. [HM]

CARMICHAEL, RACHEL, was granted patent of denization on 5 July 1631. [CPRI]

CARMICHAEL, WILLIAM, a soldier of Colonel Bayley's Regiment, 22 February 1648. [HMC.Ormonde.ii.70]

CARR HENRY, an Ensign of the Earl of Dunbarton's Regiment which landed at Kinsale in April 1679. [HMC.Ormonde.ii.219]

CARR, JOHN, born 1632, died 24 July 1711. [Donaghcloney gravestone, County Down]

CARR, ROBERT, a Lieutenant of the Earl of Dunbarton's Regiment which landed at Kinsale in April 1679. [HMC.Ormonde.ii.219]

CARR, THOMAS, of Ballydocke, County Down, 1663. [PRONI.T407]

CASSEN, JOHN, in County Down, 1610. [LC.1582]

CATHCART, ADAM, a gentleman in Casibcon, parish of Devonish, County Fermanagh, 1659, agent for Ludovic Hamilton. [C]

CATHCART, ALEXANDER, a gentleman in Agasillis, parish of Devonish, County Fermanagh, 1659. [C]

CATHCART, ALLAN, in Enniskillen, County Fermnagh, will refers to his wife Anna, Captain Charles Hamilton, William Hamilton an attorney, John Futon; witnesses William Roscrow and Thomas Roscrow both in Enniskillen, Charles Hamilton a gentleman in Belcoo, County Fermanagh, and John Cathcart, probate 8 May 1721. [DRD]

CATHCART, GABRIEL, a gentleman in Tulliscanlon, parish of Devonish, County Fermanagh, 1659. [C]

CATHCART, JAMES, in Ballyenyane, Member of the Irish Parliament for the borough of Newton Ards in 1613. [MM]

CATHCART, JAMES, a landowner in Ulster, 22 June 1627. [CPRI]

CATHCART, ROBERT, a gentleman in Drumnadown, parish of Devonish, County Fermanagh, 1659. [C]

CAUDEN, WILLIAM, a tenant in Hollywood Town, County Down, in 1681. [HM]

CAUL, JAMES, a tenant in Hollywood Town, County Down, in 1681. [HM]

CAUL, ..., a widow, a tenant in Hollywood Town, County Down, in 1681. [HM]

CHAMBERS, JAMES, in Belfast, a will, 1681. [PRONI.T700.1]

CHALMERS, JOHN, a Presbyterian, a merchant and a burgess of Belfast from 1693 to his death in 1708. [BMF]

CHAMBERS, JAMES, a tenant in Hollywood Town, County Down, in 1681. [HM]

CHARTERS, ROBERT, a Lieutenant of the Earl of Dunbarton's Regiment which landed at Kinsale in April 1679. [HMC.Ormonde.ii.219]

CHRISTIE, GEORGE, son of James Christie, minister at Omagh, County Tyrone, a sasine 26 May 1730. [NRS.RS23.11/8]

CLARKE, ANDREW, a tenant in Bangor town, County Down, 1681. [HM]

CLELAND, JOHN, a tenant in Bangor town, County Down, 1681. [HM]

CLELAND, PATRICK, a tenant in Bangor town, County Down, in 1681. [HM]

CLELAND, ..., a widow, a tenant in Bangor town, County Down, in 1681. [HM]

CLERKE, DAVID, a Lieutenant of the Earl of Dunbarton's Regiment which landed at Kinsale in April 1679. [HMC.Ormonde.ii.219]

CLERK, WILLIAM, a merchant tailor in Dublin, natural son of Robert Clerk a merchant burgess of Edinburgh, a disposition, 18 June 1684. [ECA.MB.IV.bundle 80/3514]

COCKBURN, GEORGE, an Ensign of the Earl of Dunbarton's Regiment which landed at Kinsale in April 1679. [HMC.Ormonde.ii.219]

COCKBURN, WILLIAM, was pardoned for the murder of Sir John Wemyss, 6 May 1629. [CPRI]

COLQUHOUN, MATTHEW, a soldier at Carrickfergus, a letter, 8 November 1642. [NRS.GD164.1600]

COLVILLE, ALEXANDER, Precentor of the Church of St Saviour of Connor, 8 August 1628. [CPRI]

COLVILLE, ALEXANDER, transported by Captain Bryan Fitzpatrick for service under the King of Sweden, 1630. [APCE.1630.1304]

COLVILLE, HUGH, died 7 February 1701. [Abbey Church gravestone, Newtonards]

COLVILLE, Sir ROBERT, died 12 June 1697. [Abbey Church gravestone, Newtonards]

COLVILLE, Lady ROSE, died 6 February 1693. [Abbey Church gravestone, Newtonards]

CONYNGHAM, ADAM, a Lieutenant of the Earl of Dunbarton's Regiment which landed at Kinsale in April 1679. [HMC.Ormonde.ii.219]

CONYNGHAM, ALEXANDER, a Lieutenant of the Earl of Dunbarton's Regiment which landed at Kinsale in April 1679. [HMC.Ormonde.ii.219]

CONINGHAM, CUTHBERT, in County Down, 1610. [LC.1582]

CONSTABLE, ROBERT, master of the Mary at Limerick, 24 December 1642. [NRS.GD52.106]

COOPER, ..., a widow, a tenant in Hollywood Town, County Down, in 1681. [HM]

CORREY, JOHN, a tenant in Hollywood Town, County Down, in 1681. [HM]

COULTER, CHRISTOPHER, master of the Katherine of Ardglass, 1615. [UPB.102]

COULTER, JOHN, a surgeon on Island McGhie, 1686, a petition. [NRS.JP36.5.1]

COUTIES, ROBERT, agent for Bernard and Robert

Lindsay undertakers, resident in the Precinct of Mountjoy in 1611. [Carew Mss.58]

COWIE, ..., a widow, a tenant in Hollywood Town, County Down, in 1681. [HM]

CRAFFORD, HENRY, a gentleman in Sligo town, Barony of Carbry, County Sligo, in 1659. [C]

CRAFORD, Major JAMES, in the parish of Ballyniskrean, Londonderry, 1659. [C]

CRAFFORD, WILLIAM, a gentleman in Ballibun, parish of Donoghmore, Barony of Raphoe, County Donegal, 1659. [C]

CRAFORD, WILLIAM, a tenant in Part Killare near Bangor, County Down, in 1681. [HM]

CRAFORD, WILLIAM, a Presbyterian, a merchant and a burgess of Belfast from 1687 to his death in 1707. [BMF]

CRAFFORD, WILLIAM, in Belfast, County Antrim, will refers to his wife Janet, his son and heir David Crafford, his grand-children William Crafford and Anne Crafford, his daughter Helenor and her husband Roger Haddock, grandson John Haddock, sister Grissell McCologh a widow, George MacCartney in Belfast, Reverend John Kirpatrick, Robert Donaldson an attorney, Robert Stevenson and Hugh Moore; witnesses John Chalmers a merchant, Benjamin Paterson a merchant, William King servant to Samuel McClintock an innkeeper in Belfast, John Jameson, and David Crafford, probate 11 October 1716. [DRD]

CRAIG, DANIEL, in Ballybrack, Ballymoney, 1720. [UJA.VII.10]

CRAIG, HUGH, a shopkeeper in Coleraine, 1659. [C]

CRAIG, JAMES, deputy of John Auchmuty and Alexander Auchmuty, resident in the Precinct of Tullaghchinko in 1611. [Carew.Mss.58]

CRAIG, Sir JAMES, and his wife Dame Mary, were granted 2000 acres in the barony of Tolloghconcho, County Cavan, to be known as the Manor of Castlecraig on 26 April 1631. [CPRI]

CRAIG, JOHN, a merchant in Diamond Street, Londonderry, 1659. [C]

CRAIG, ROBERT, son of John Craig, a merchant in County Antrim, a deed, 1715. [NRS.RD3.145.543]

CRAWFORD, ALEXANDER, at Carrickfergus, 7 June 1648. [NRS.GD406.1.7338]

CRAWFORD, GEORGE, of Loughnorrice, Rathlin Island, 1617. [Carew mss.1817.183]

CRAWFORD, PATRICK, of Raloo, born 1718, died 22 May 1801, husband of Anne Drummond, born 1718, died 13 March 1789. [Raloo gravestone, County Antrim]

CRAWFORD, WILLIAM, a gentleman in Ballymullen, parish of Bangor, Barony of the Ards, County Down, 1659. [C]

CRAWFORD, WILLIAM, a gentleman in Ballemullan, parish of Bangor, Barony of the Ards, County Down, 1659. [C]

CREIGHTON, ABRAHAM, a gentleman in Crum, parish of Drumully, County Fermanagh, 1659. [C]

CREICHTON, JOHN, in Ireland, heir to John Creichton of Achlean, brother of Robert Creichton alias Murray of

Gladmoor, 13 February 1724. [ECA.MBVI.bundle 175/6906] [NRS.S/H.18.2.1724]

CREIGHTON, JAMES, was licenced to dispose of land in County Leitrim to Thomas Abercrombie, 30 November 1631. [CPRI]

CREICHTON, JOHN, in Crum, County Fermanagh, will refers to David Creichton of Lifford, County Donegal, his eldest son Abraham Creichton, sister Mary Creichton, aunt Marianna Willoughby, Sir Gustavus Hume, Sir Ralph Gore, Brigadier David Creichton, Hugh Willoughby, James Hamilton in Brownhall, and his brother Abraham Hamilton; witnesses Robert Hamilton, Robert Richardson, William Armstrong, Charles Crenar in Dublin, Thomas Burgh, and Abraham Hamilton, probate 14 January 1716. [DRD]

CREIGHTON, THOMAS, agent for Lord D'Aubigny, in the Precinct of Clanchie in 1611. [Carew.Mss.58]

CRIGHTON, JAMES, a gentleman, in Castle Murray, parish of Killagtie, Barony of Boylagh and Banagh, County Donegal, 1659. [C]

CRINGLE, JAMES, a tenant in Ballywaltertown, County Down, 1681. [HM]

CRISWELL, HUGH, a tenant in Hollywood Town, County Down, in 1681. [HM]

CRISWELL, JAMES, sr., a tenant in Hollywood Town, County Down, in 1681. [HM]

CRISWELL, WILLIAM, a tenant in Hollywood Town, County Down, in 1681. [HM]

CUMIN, JOHN, tenant in Ballylisbredan, County Down, in 1681. [HM]

CUNNINGHAM, ALEXANDER, minister of Inver, County Donegal, 5 June 1625; prebend of Invernally, County Donegal, was appointed Bishop of Raphoe in 1629. [NRS.GD3.2.29.8] [CPRI]

CUNNINGHAM, ALEXANDER, in town of Letterkenny, parish of Cornwall, Barony of Killmccrenan, County Donegal, 1659. [C]

CUNNINGHAM, ALEXANDER, in Belliara, parish of Killebeggs, Barony of Boylagh and Banagh, County Donegal, 1659. [C]

CUNNINGHAM, ANDREW, in Belliara, parish of Killebeggs, Barony of Boylagh and Banagh, County Donegal, 1659. [C]

CUNNINGHAM, CUTHBERT, residing in the Precinct of Portlogh in 1611. [Carew.Mss.58]

CUNNINGHAM, GEORGE, in Loughriscoll, Member of the Irish Parliament for the borough of Newton Ards in 1613. [MM]

CUNNINGHAM, GEORGE, a gentleman in Tamnitullen township, parish of Inver, Barony of Boylagh and Banagh, County Donegal, 1659. [C]

CUNNINGHAM, JAMES, was granted denization and 1000 acres in the barony of Raphoe, County Donegal, to be called the Manor of Fort Cunningham, 29 May 1629. [CPRI]

CUNNINGHAM, JAMES, in town of Letterkenny, parish of Cornwall, Barony of Killmccrenan, County Donegal, 1659. [C]

CUNNINGHAM, JAMES, and his son John Cunningham, in Belliaghan, parish of Ray, Barony of Raphoe, County Donegal, 1659. [C]

CUNNINGHAM, JOHN, of Cranfield, residing in the Precinct of Portlogh in 1611. [Carew.mss58]

CUNNINGHAM, JOHN, was granted denization and 2000 acres in the precinct of Portlogh, County Donegal, to be called the Manor of Castle Cunningham, 29 May 1629. [CPRI]

CUNNINGHAM, JOHN, a gentleman in Tully, parish of Tully, Barony of Killmccrenan, County Donegal, 1659. [C]

CUNNINGHAM, JOHN, a gentleman in Drumfad, parish of Donaghadee, Barony of The Ards, County Down, in 1659. [C]

CUNNINGHAM, JOHN, master of the Prosperity of Sligo, from Ayr to Belfast or Dundalk in 1689. [RPCS.XIV.588/599]

CUNNINGHAM, JOHN, of Crochan near Londonderry, a petitioner, 1689. [RPCS.XIII.392]

CUNNINGHAM, Lady KATHERINE, was granted denization on 17 August 1627. [CPRI]

CUNNINGHAM, ROBERT, master of the Janet of Mongavlin, 1614. [UPB.6]

CUNNINGHAM, ROBERT, a gentleman in Ballysallagh, parish of Bangor, barony of the Ards, County Down, 1659. [C]

CUNNINGHAM, ROBERT, a gentleman in Ballylidie, parish of Bangor, barony of The Ards, County Down, 1659. [C]

CUNNINGHAM, ROBERT, a tenant in Castlespick, Manor of Ballydeine, County Down, 1681. [HM]

CUNNINGHAM, WILLIAM, probably in County Donegal, was granted letters of denization, 19 July 1631. [CPRI]

CUNNINGHAM, WILLIAM, a gentleman in Tamnitullen township, parish of Inver, Barony of Boylagh and Banagh, County Donegal, 1659. [C]

CUNNINGHAM, WILLIAM, a gentleman in Monfad, parish of Taghboine, County Donegal, 1659. [C]

CUNNINGHAM, WILLIAM, a gentleman in Plaister, parish of Taghboine, County Donegal, 1659. [C]

DALZIELL, JAMES, in Ballyglighorn, Manor of Ballydeine, County Down, 1681. [HM]

DARAGH, ARCHIBALD, born 1717, died 11 April 1762, father of John Daragh, died 15 August 1745 aged one year, and Esther Daragh, died 22 May 1744 aged two years. [Bun-na-margie Friary gravestone, Antrim]

DAVISON, JOHN, a tenant in Bangor town, County Down, in 1681. [HM]

DAWSON, JAMES, and his spouse Margaret Wyllie, servants at Lisburn Castle, County Antrim, thieves who fled to Dunfermline, Fife, to be returned to Ireland for trial, 1690. [RPCS.XV.25]

DELAP. JAMES, a gentleman, in Crogan, parish of Auchnish, Barony of Killmccrenan, County Donegal, 1659. [C]

DELAP, JOHN, a tenant in Ballywaltertown, County Down, 1681. [HM]

DENHAM, JOHN, son of Robert Denham of West Shiels in Scotland, in the town lands of Ballebegin, parish of Dundonell, County Down, indenture by James, Lord Viscount Clausboye, a Lord of HM Council of Estates in Ireland, 12 September 1612. [NRS.GD3.14.1.27]

DENISON, ..., a widow, a tenant in Hollywood Town, County Down, in 1681. [HM]

DENNISTON, GEORGE, a merchant in Dublin, his will refers to his wife Jane Craig or Denniston, his son William Denniston, his daughter Margaret Dennison; witnesses William Johnston at Finglass Bridge, County Dublin, Barnaby Rider a servant dwelling on Ormand Quay, Dublin, and Eu. Lavery, probate 8 May 1718. [DRD]

DENNY, JOHN, a merchant in Pomp Street, Londonderry, 1659. [C]

DICKSON, JOHN, born 1666, died 27 September 1728. [Blaris gravestone, County Down]

DIXON, ANDREW, tenant in the Church Quarter of Dundonell, County Down, in 1681. [HM]

DOAKE, HUGH, a Presbyterian, a merchant and a burgess of Belfast from 1642 to 1669. [BMF]

DOBBY, ALEXANDER, a tenant in Bangor town, County Down, 1681. [HM]

DOCK, JAMES, in Ireland, was served heir to John Dock a smith burgess of Ayr 'his guidsir brother son' on 22 August 1654, [NRS.Retours Ayr.464]

DONALDSON, ALEXANDER, in Lubitavish, County Antrim, will, 1666. [PRONI.T700.1]

DONALDSON, HUGH, in Ballymoney, a will, 1683. [PRONI.T700.1]

DONALDSON, JOHN, in Glenarine, Ireland, a bond, 23 September 1661. [NRS.RD2.2.583]

DOUGLAS, ANDREW, born in Glasgow, a skipper who settled in Coleraine, County Londonderry, around 1679, master of the Phoenix of Londonderry carried refugees from Belfast and Antrim to Scotland. In 1689 he was licenced as a privateer. [RPCS.XIII. 389]

DOUGLAS, ARCHIBALD, a Captain of the Earl of Dunbarton's Regiment which landed at Kinsale in April 1679. [HMC.Ormonde.ii.219]

DOUGLAS, Reverend CHARLES, born 1743, Prebendary of Connor 1781-1813, died 30 June 1833. [Derryveighan gravestone, County Antrim]

DOUGLAS, ROBERT, a Captain of the Earl of Dunbarton's Regiment which landed at Kinsale in April 1679. [HMC.Ormonde.ii.219]

DOUGLAS, Sir WILLIAM, a Captain of the Earl of Dunbarton's Regiment which was landed at Kinsale in April 1679, and later in Iniskene. [HMC.Ormonde.ii.219]

DRUMMOND, MALCOLM, was granted denization and 1000 acres in the barony of Strabane, County Tyrone, to be called the manor of Castle Drummond, 29 May 1629. [CPRI]

DRUMMOND, THOMAS, a non-conformist minister in Ireland, petitioned King Charles II in 1669. [CSPI]

DUDGEON, RICHARD, a merchant in Dublin, and James

Dudgeon a merchant burgess of Inverkeithing, Fife, 20 April 1698. [NRS.GD10.842]

DUFF, GEORGE, a linen draper in Dublin, his will refers to his wife Dorothy, his brothers-in-law William Boyes and Richard Boyes; witnesses James Boyes son of said William Boyes, Thomas Smith servant to said Dorothy Duff, John Smith a Notary Public in Dublin, James Wilkie clerk to Brien Worthington a Notary Public in Dublin, and James Bowden, probate 3 November 1720. [DRD]

DUNBAR, ALEXANDER, a resident of the Precinct of Boylagh in 1611. [Carew.Mss.58]

DUNBAR, DAVID, in Kerucastle, parish of Auchnish, Barony of Killmccrenan, County Donegal, 1659. [C]

DUNBAR, JAMES, a tenant in Bangor town, County Down, 1681. [HM]

DUNBAR, ROBERT, was presented to the Prebend of Rasarhan in the Cathedral of Connor, 25 November 1628. [CPRI]

DUNBAR, WILLIAM, a gentleman in Beagh, parish of Ennismcsaint, County Fermanagh, 1659. [C]

DUNBAR, ..., in County Fermanagh, 1611. [Carew mss.1611.68]

DUNCAN, JOHN, ["Jan Doncken"], an Irish soldier, married Anne Thomson, ["Anneke Taemssen"], from Scotland, widow of William Livingston, ["Willem Lieviston"], in Leiden, Holland, 11 July 1603. [Leiden Marriage Register]

DUNDAS, HUGH, a gentleman in the townlands of Clontene Kelly, County Down, 1659. [C]

DUNGAN, ..., a widow, a tenant in Ballywaltertown, County Down, 1681. [HM]

DUNDAS, JOHN, born 1652, died 5 February 1737. [Baldoyle gravestone, County Dublin]

DUNLOP, JOHN, a tenant in Bangor town, County Down, 1681. [HM]

DUNLOP, JOHN, tenant in the Church Quarter of Dundonell, County Down, in 1681. [HM]

ECCLES, GILBERT, a gentleman in Shannock, County Fermanagh, in 1659. [C]

ECCLES, HUGH, a Presbyterian, a merchant and a burgess of Belfast from 1667 to 1681. [BMF]

ECCLES, JOSEPH, in Rathmoran, County Fermanagh, will refers to his only brother Charles Eccles of Fintonagh, County Tyrone; Hugh Raney; witnesses Luke Stanford a gentleman in Belturbet, County Cavan, Moses Richards a gentleman, Thomas Ashe in Magherafelt, County Londonderry, William Balfour, Joseph Caldwell, and John Kerr all of Lisnkee, County Fermanagh, John Buchanan, John Creery, and James Wachup, all in Fintonagh, County Tyrone, probate 24 May 1723. [DRD]

ECHLIN, HENRY, in Dublin, a lease, 1686. [PRONI.D69.1]

ECHLIN, HENRY, in Ahoghill, a will, 1728. [PRONI.T700.1]

ECHLIN, ROBERT, born 1635, died 20 December 1706. [St John's, gravestone]

ECHLIN, ROBERT, in Rush, Member of the Irish Parliament for the borough of Newton Ards in 1692. [MM]

EDGAR, HUGH, of Ballytibbert, Barony of Dunluce, 1720. [UJA.VII.9]

EDMONDS, ARCHIBALD, servant to George Campbell in Canwell, Ireland, a witness, 1662. [NRS.Argyll Sasines, vol.iv.1060]

EDMONDSTON, ARCHIBALD, son and heir of William Edmondston of Broad Island, Antrim, 1 September 1628. [CPRI]

EDMONDSTON, ARCHIBALD, was pardoned of the alienation of lands in County Antrim to Randal, Earl of Antrim, 27 June 1631. [CPRI]

EDMONDSTON, ARCHIBALD, of Ballybrian, was granted patent of denization on 5 July 1631. [CPRI]

ELLIOTT, ROBERT, a gentleman in Targin, parish of Dumully, County Fermanagh, 1659. [C]

ENNIS, ALEXANDER, a Lieutenant of the Earl of Dunbarton's Regiment which landed at Kinsale in April 1679. [HMC.Ormonde.ii.219]

ENNIS, ROBERT, a Lieutenant of the Earl of Dunbarton's Regiment which landed at Kinsale in April 1679. [HMC.Ormonde.ii.219]

ERSKINE, ALEXANDER, Rector of Devenish, County Fermanagh, lands in the Barony of Magheraboy, County Fermanagh, 29 February 1631. [CPRI]

ERSKINE, ARCHIBALD, Rector of Inishysawe, was granted lands in the Barony of Magheraboy, 29 February 1631. [CPRI]

ERSKINE, JAMES, was granted 3450 acres in the Barony of

Clogher, County Tyrone, to be called the Manor of Favor Royall, 12 July 1630. [CPRI]

ERSKINE, JAMES, in Bogay, parish of Aghnunshen, Barony of Killmccrenan, County Donegal, 1659. [C]

EWING, ALEXANDER, in town of Letterkenny, parish of Cornwall, Barony of Killmccrenan, County Donegal, 1659. [C]

FERGUSON, HUGH, a tenant in Tullenkill, Manor of Ballydeine, County Down, 1681. [HM]

FERGUSON, JOHN, a gentleman in Cloghfin, County Sligo, 1659. [C]

FERGUSON, THOMAS, a tenant in Bangor town, County Down, 1681. [HM]

FINLAY, ALEXANDER, a soldier of Colonel Bayley's Regiment, 22 February 1648. [HMC.Ormonde.ii.69]

FINLAY, ANDREW, a tenant in Bangor town, County Down, in 1681. [HM]

FINLAY, JOHN, the elder, a soldier of Colonel Bayley's Regiment, 22 February 1648. [HMC.Ormonde.ii.69]

FINLAY, JOHN, the younger, a soldier of Colonel Bayley's Regiment, 22 February 1648. [HMC.Ormonde.ii.69]

FINLAY, ROBERT, a soldier of Colonel Bayley's Regiment, 22 February 1648. [HMC.Ormonde.ii.69]

FLEMING, ANNA, daughter of John Fleming of Coltston a merchant in Glasgow, wife of Colonel William Pinkston, Coast Officer at Donaghadee, died 12 July 1727. [FIB.II.388]

FLEMING, JAMES, son of Alexander Fleming, rector of

Ramochy or Ray, County Donegal, in 1660, died in 1684; he married Janet, daughter of Reverend Alexander Forsyth of Letterkenny, County Donegal. [FIB.II.356]

FLEMING, JOHN, in the parish of Mevagh, Barony of Kilmccrenan, County Donegal, 1659. [C]

FLEMING, ROBERT, a gentleman in Collidue, parish of Movill, Barony of Killmccrenan, County Donegal, 1659. [C]

FLEMING, WILLIAM, a merchant in Leith, to move to Ireland with his family, 12 March 1658. [Edinburgh Burgh Records]

FLETCHER, HENRY, was appointed Captain, Commander of Ballinefadd Fort, County Sligo, with ten men, 17 June 1628. [CPRI]

FORBES, Sir ARTHUR, in Ireland, 21 October 1628. [CPRI]

FORREST, GEORGE, a tenant in Hollywood Town, County Down, in 1681. [HM]

FORRESTER, ELIZABETH, daughter of Mr Alexander Forrester a clerk in Londonderry, was granted a Crown Charter of the Halls of Airth, Stirlingshire, on 14 August 1700. [NRS.RGS.15.15]

FORSYTH, MARION, relict of Reverend John Crichton of Christ Church, Dublin, mother of Captain William Crichton spouse of Jean Hamilton, a bond, 1675. [NRS.GD45.16.2522]

FORSYTH, NATHANIEL, a tenant in Bangor town, County Down, 1681. [HM]

FORTANCE, JAMES, was pardoned for the murder of Sir John Wemyss, 6 May 1629. [CPRI]

FRASER, JOHN, of Cappy, born 1613, died 1711, father of John, Robert, Rob and Patrick. [Seapatrick gravestone] [HMC.Ormonde.ii.70]

FRASER, JOHN, of Dromore, born 1712, died 19 September 1778. [Domore Cathedral gravestone, County Down]

FRAZER, ROBERT, died in August 17-0, husband of Jane, born 1676, died 1746. [Dromore Cathedral gravestone, County Down]

FULLERTON, Sir JAMES, was granted land in County Donegal, 27 June 1628. [CPRI]

FULLERTON, JOHN, agent for James Douglas in the Precinct of Clanchie in 1611. [Carew.Mss.58]

FULLERTON, WILLIAM, Rector of Rossurrir, was granted lands in the Barony of Magheraboy on 29 February 1631. [CPRI]

FULLERTON, WILLIAM, clerk and Archdeacon of Armagh and Prebend of Carncastle, died September 166-, and his wife Jean, daughter of Robert Echlin, the Bishop of Down and Connor, parents of Robert, William, John, Jean, Margaret, Euphame, Isobel, Mary, and Agnes. [Derryveighen gravestone, County Antrim]

FULLERTON, WILLIAM, a tenant in Hollywood Town, County Down, in 1681. [HM]

FULTON, JOHN, in Letra, County Fermanagh, 1659. [C]

GALBREATH, ANDREW, a gentleman in Tullyvoile, parish of Enniskeane, County Fermanagh, 1659. [C]

GALBRAITH, HUGH, a merchant in Dublin, 1692. [NRS.GDE41.20]

GALBRAITH, HUMPHREY, was pardoned for the murder of Sir John Wemyss, 6 May 1629. [CPRI]

GALBRAITH, JAMES, in Claghmoran, County Fermanagh, in 1659. [C]

GALBREATH, ROBERT, a gentleman in Tullyvoile, parish of Enniskeane, County Fermanagh, 1659. [C]

GALBRAITH, ROBERT, in Dowish, parish of Ray, Barony of Raphoe, County Donegal, 1659. [C]

GALBRAITH, ROBERT, son and heir of the late John Galbraith in Blessingburn, County Tyrone, grandchild of Archibald Galbraith, 8 October 1678. [NRS.GD220.1.13.3.6]

GALBRAITH, WILLIAM, was pardoned for the murder of Sir John Wemyss, 6 May 1629. [CPRI]

GALLOWAY, ELIZA, born 1703, died 5 January 1778. [Dromara gravestone, County Down]

GALT, JOHN, a shopkeeper in Coleraine, 1659. [C]

GALT.JOHN, in Coleraine, a will, 1700. [PRONI.T700.1]

GALT, WILLIAM, a shopkeeper in Coleraine, 1659. [C]

GAMBLE, JOHN, a tenant in Hollywood Town, County Down, in 1681. [HM]

GARDNER, JOHN, in Barony of Loughty, County Cavan, 1630. [BL.Add.MS.4770]

GARDNER, THOMAS, master of the Alice of Londonderry, captured by Parliamentary forces when bound from Londonderry to Chester, England, in 1643. [TNA.HCA.13.61.176]

GARDNER, WILLIAM, in Barony of Loughty, County Cavan, 1630. [BL.Add.MS.4770]

GARTHLAND, J., in Carrickfergus, a letter, 29 June 1648. [NRS.GD406.1.2283]

GARVEN, HUGH, a tenant in Bangor town, County Down, 1681. [HM]

GARVEN, THOMAS, master of the Jennett of Belfast, captured by Parliamentary forces when bound from Bordeaux, France, to Carrickfergus in 1644. [TNA.HCA.13.59.204]

GASTLE, WILLIAM, a tenant in Bangor town, County Down, in 1681. [HM]

GAY, JOHN, a tenant in Ballywaltertown, County Down, 1681. [HM]

GIBB, JAMES, a gentleman, was granted land in County West Meath, 9 March 1626. [CPRI]

GIBBON, JOHN, a tenant in Hollywood Town, County Down, in 1681. [HM]

GIBSON, JOHN, master of the Mayflower of Dublin, from Belfast to Dublin, 1685. [NRS.JC39.87]

GIBSON, WILLIAM, a tenant in Bangor town, County Down, in 1681. [HM]

GIBSON,......., a widow, a tenant in Ballywaltertown, County Down, in 1681. [HM]

GILMORE, JOHN, formerly of Gabrochill, Stewarton parish, Ayrshire, thereafter in Ireland, a deed, 1623. [NRAS.3957.7]

GILMORE, JOHN, a tenant in Bangor town, County Down, 1681. [HM]

GILPATRICK, JOHN, a tenant in Bangor town, County Down, 1681. [HM]

GLASGOW, JAMES, master of the James of Belfast from 1661 to 1675. [BMF.130]

GLASS, WILLIAM, in Lislagan, Ballymoney, 1720. [UJA.VII.10]

GLASS, WILLIAM, in the Barony of Kilconway, 1720. [UJA.VII.11]

GLEN, WILLIAM, in Maghremenagh, Liberty of Coleraine, 1720. [UJA.VII.10]

GLENDINNING, ROBERT, a gentleman, was granted land in County West Meath, 9 March 1626. [CPRI]

GOODLAT, WILLIAM, in Derrygall, John Bovell, parish of Killiman, County Tyrone, will refers to his nephew William Richardson of Mulloghatinhy, County Armagh, his niece Jane Richardson, and his grand-nephew Thomas Richardson; witnesses Symon Haselton a gentleman in the parish of Killiman County Tyrone, John Bovell a weaver in the parish of

Clonfecle, and William Haselton a gentleman in Bovean, County Tyrone, Andrew Carmichael in Dungannon, County Tyrone, probate Armagh, 24 March 1727. [DRD]

GORDON, JOHN, died 1710. [Raloo gravestone, County Antrim]

GORDON, ROBERT, a Lieutenant of the Earl of Dunbarton's Regiment at Kinsale in April 1679. [HMC.Ormonde.ii.219]

GORDON, ROBERT, deceased, son and heir of the late Sir Robert Gordon, with lands in County Longford, 9 March 1626. [CPRI]

GOWAN, or SMITH, DANIEL, in the townlands of Ballyidocks, County Down, 1659. [C]

GOWDY, JOHN, a schoolmaster, a tenant in Bangor town, County Down, 1681. [HM]

GOWDY, WILLIAM, a tenant in Tullivastilanagh, County Down, 1681. [HM]

GRAHAM, ARTHUR, in Bullecullan, parish of Dumally, County Fermanagh, 1659. [C]

GRAHAM, GEORGE, a Lieutenant of the Earl of Dunbarton's Regiment which landed at Kinsale in April 1679. [HMC.Ormonde.ii.219]

GRAHAM, WILLIAM, the Muster Master for the Provinces of Leinster and Ulster, 29 September 1628. [CPRI]

GRAHAM, WILLIAM, in Dublin, a letter, 1631. [NRS.GD22.3.589]

GRASSICK, DONALD, in Salloquhar, Strabane, 21 October 1652. [NRS.GD38.1.197]

GREER, ..., a widow, a tenant in Bangor town, County Down, 1681. [HM]

GREG, ANDREW, a merchant in Donaghadee, 1692. [NRS.AC7.9]

GREG, JOHN, a gentleman in Castle Murray, parish of Killagtie, Barony of Boylagh and Banagh, County Donegal, 1659. [C]

GREGG, JOHN, master of the Adventure of Belfast in 1661. [BMF.130]

GREG, ..., a widow, a tenant in Ballywaltertown, County Down, 1681. [HM]

GROSSET, GREGORY, from Enniskilling, and Elizabeth Atkinson, were married in the Presbyterian Church in Rotterdam, The Netherlands, on 14 June 1711. [GAR]

HAIR, JOHN, of Listabill in Ireland, a deed, 1672. [NRS.RD2.31.635]

HALL, EDWARD, master aboard the John of Carrickfergus, from La Rochelle, France, to Carrickfergus, 1615. [UPB]

HAMILL, HUGH, tenant of Ballyatwood, County Down, in 1681. [HM]

HAMILL, HUGH, a tenant in Ballywaltertown, County Down, in 1681. [HM]

HAMILL, HUGH, a tenant in Ballyrasely, County Down, 1681. [HM]

HAMILTON, Captain ALEXANDER, born 1613, died 1648, second son of Patrick Hamilton of Innerwick in Scotland, husband of Mary Reading, parents of Patrick, Mary, and Elizabeth. [Old Abbey Church gravestone, Bangor, County Down]

HAMILTON, ALEXANDER, a tenant in Ballyvernon near Bangor, County Down, in 1681. [HM]

HAMILTON, ANN, daughter of James Hamilton late of Neilsbrook, County Antrim, a deed, 1694. [PRONI.D74.1]

HAMILTON, ARCHIBALD, was denizised and granted the manor of Moyenner, in March 1628. [CPRI]

HAMILTON, ARCHIBALD, Bishop of Killala and Ardconragh, was translated to the Archbishopric of Cashel and bishopric of Emly, 20 April 1630. [CPRI]

HAMILTON, ARCHIBALD, in Killeleagh townlands, County Down, 159. [C]

HAMILTON, ARCHIBALD, a tenant in Bangor town, County Down, 1681. [HM]

HAMILTON, ARCHIBALD, a tenant in Part Killare near Bangor, County Down, in 1681. [HM]

HAMILTON, ARCHIBALD, a tenant in Ballywaltertown, County Down, in 1681. [HM]

HAMILTON, ARCHIBALD, a tenant in Ballykeels, County Down, 1681. [HM]

HAMILTON, ARCHIBALD, tenant of Dunlady, Hollywood, County Down, in 1681. [HM]

HAMILTON, CLAUDE, resident in the Precinct of Tullaghchinko in 1611, son of Sir Alexander Hamilton. [Carew. Mss.58]

HAMILTON, Sir FRANCIS, was granted land in the Barony of Tullochoncho, County Cavan, to be known as the Manor of Castlekeylaghe, 17 June 1631. [CPRI]

HAMILTON, FRANCIS, in Clontenorin, County Fermanagh, 1659. [C]

HAMILTON, Captain FRANCIS, a gentleman in Kilmure, parish of Taghboine, Barony of Raphoe, County Donegal, 1659. [C]

HAMILTON, Sir FREDERICK, was appointed member of a commission to try by martial law offences committed by the 50th Regiment of Foot, 28 June 1627. [CPRI]

HAMILTON, Lieutenant GAWEN, tenant of Ballyhackamore and Tollyard, Hollywood, County Down, in 1681. [HM]

HAMILTON, GAWEN, a tenant in Lisleen, Hollywood town, County Down, in 1681. [HM]

HAMILTON, GAVIN, of Lisowin, County Down, a deed, 1694. [PRONI.D74.1]

HAMILTON, GAVIN, born 1640, died 1718, father of Gavin Hamilton, born 1701, died 1720, William Hamilton, born 1700, died 1772. [Dromore Cathedral gravestone, County Down]

HAMILTON, Sir GEORGE, licenced to hold markets at Clogher, County Tyrone, 7 February 1631. [CPRI]

HAMILTON, Sir GEORGE, Commissary General, the accounts for 1689. [NRS.E91.3/20-23]; born 1666 in Hamilton, Lanarkshire, son of the Duke of Hamilton, he was Colonel of the Inniskilling Regiment of Foot and fought at the battles of the Boyne and Aughrim in 1690. [SP.VI.578]

HAMILTON, GILBERT, of Dunlady, Ireland, a deed 1714. [NRS.RD2.103.1.623]

HAMILTON, GUSTAVUS, in Croghan, parish of Lifford, Barony of Raphoe, County Donegal, 1659. [C]

HAMILTON, Sir HANS, of Hamilton's Bawn, County Armagh, a lease, 1686. [PRONI.D69.1]

HAMILTON, HUGH, a tenant in Ballywaltertown, County Down, 1681. [HM]

HAMILTON, HUGH, tenant of Ganway, County Down, in 1681. [HM]

HAMILTON, HUGH, a tenant in Bangor town, County Down, 1681. [HM]

HAMILTON, JAMES, son of Malcolm Hamilton, Lord Archbishop of Cashel, 17 July 1626. [CPRI]

HAMILTON, JAMES, of Ballywalter, County Dow, was granted patent of denization on 5 July 1631. [CPRI]

HAMILTON, JAMES, a merchant and Provost of Bangor, died 21 January 1649. [Old Abbey Church gravestone, Bangor, County Down]

HAMILTON, JAMES, in the townlands of Saule and Ballysugach, County Down, in 1659. [C]

HAMILTON, JAMES, in Killeleagh Castle Townlands, County Down, 1659. [C]

HAMILTON, JAMES, a gentleman in Fentraugh townland, parish of Killebeggs, Barony of Boylagh and Banagh, County Donegal, 1659. [C]

HAMILTON, JAMES, in Saule and Ballysugh, in the parish of Down, Barony of Lecale, County Down, 1659. [C]

HAMILTON, JAMES, a tenant in Ballywaltertown, County Down, 1681. [HM]

HAMILTON, JAMES, a tenant in Ballygilbert near Bangor, County Down, in 1681. [HM]

HAMILTON, JAMES, a tenant in Bangor town, County Down, 1681. [HM]

HAMILTON, JAMES, tenant of Ballycleghan, Hollywood, County Down, in 1681. [HM]

HAMILTON, JAMES, of Newcastle, County Down, a lease, 1686. [PRONI.D69.1]

HAMILTON, JAMES, in Court Hills, County Meath, will refers to his wife, Edward Hamilton, 'the children of his sisters Margaret Mary and Jane Hamilton', his brother Colonel Andrew Hamilton, Andrew Teate, and Richard Dudgeon, witnesses were John Christian a gentleman in Dublin, Hugh Gillespy and William Henderson both yeomen in Court Hills, also William Hogan, 7 January 1708. [DRD]

HAMILTON, JAMES, in Ballinegarvie, County Antrim, will refers to Rose Hamilton his wife, their children John, Rachel and William, his cousin William Hamilton of Mount Hamilton, Euphemia Cunningham, Robert Hamilton a merchant in Strabane, his brother John Hamilton of of Crebilly, Ballyholly in County Londonderry, Henry O'Hara, Patrick Orr of Carnbeg. Captain William Hamilton of Coshandun, Henry Shaw in Ballygelly, Thomas Weir of Hamilton's Grove, William McGee, David Cochran of Maddykill, County Antrim, probate 7 May 1728. [DRD]

HAMILTON, JANET, spouse of John Leslie of Killiclunie, parish of Dunochade, County Cork, a bond, 27 November 1661. [NRS.RD4.3.831]

HAMILTON, JOHN, agent for Sir Claud Hamilton in County Cavan in 1611, [Carew.Mss.58]; was granted land in the barony of Clanchie, County Cavan, and lands in the Barony of Fues, County Armagh to be called the Manor of Johnstowne alias Drumergan, 29 July 1629. [CPRI]

HAMILTON, JOHN, of Loughesk, County Donegal, was granted letters of denization, 19 July 1631. [CPRI]

HAMILTON, JOHN, a gentleman in Cavan, parish of Donoghmore, Barony of Raphoe, County Donegal, 1659. [C]

HAMILTON, JOHN, a gentleman in Ballymcgowne, parish of Ballywalter, Barony of The Ards, County Down, in 1659. [C]

HAMILTON, JOHN, a gentleman in Shanon and Drumleer, parish of Lifford, Barony of Raphoe, County Donegal, 1659. [C]

HAMILTON, JOHN, in Tullicrivy, parish of Devonish, County Fermanagh, 1659. [C]

HAMILTON, JOHN, tenant of Ballymenacht, Hollywood, County Down, in 1681. [HM]

HAMILTON, JOHN, a tenant in Ballymenastragh near Bangor, County Down, in 1681. [HM]

HAMILTON, MALCOLM, Archbishop of Cashel, granted his son Archibald lands in Fermanagh on 17 July 1626. He died 1629. [CPRI]

HAMILTON, PATRICK, of Ballygrangaghe, and Elizabeth his wife, were granted patent of denization on 5 July 1631. [CPRI]

HAMILTON, PATRICK, tenant in the Church Quarter of Dundonell, County Down, in 1681. [HM]

HAMILTON, PATRICK, tenant in Granshogh, County Down, 1681. [HM]

HAMILTON, ROBERT, was appointed to the vicarage of Donnoghle in the diocese of Cashel, and to the vicarages of Lisnovallie and Donogore in the Diocese of Ely, on 22 May 1629. [CPRI]

HAMILTON, ROBERT, a gentleman in Ballygrott and Ballyskelly, parish of Bangor, Barony of the Ards, County Down, 1659. [C]

HAMILTON, ROBERT, a gentleman in Listerderry, parish of Aghahurchur, County Fermanagh, 1659. [C]

HAMILTON, ROBERT, a gentleman in Ballygrot, parish of Bangor, Barony of The Ards, County Down, 1659. [C]

HAMILTON, ROBERT, a gentleman in Cloghfyn, parish of Donoghmore, Barony of Raphoe, County Donegal, 1659. [C]

HAMILTON, ROBERT, tenant in Drumhirk, County Down, 1681. [HM]

HAMILTON, ROBERT, a tenant in Bangor town, County Down, in 1681. [HM]

HAMILTON, ROBERT, a tailor, a tenant in Bangor town, County Down, in 1681. [HM]

HAMILTON, Sir ROBERT, of Mount Hamilton, County Armagh, a deed, 1694. [PRONI.D74.1]

HAMILTON, SAMUEL, a tenant in Bressach, County Down, 1681. [HM]

HAMILTON, WILLIAM, and his wife, now in Strabane, parents of James Hamilton a burgess of Glasgow, a sasine, 20 June 1620. [NRS.B48.18.140]

HAMILTON, WILLIAM, 'a Scotsman born in Donegal, testament, 17 November 1627 Rotterdam, the Netherlands, reference to his half-brother Dick Beton. [GAR.ONA.188.73/111]

HAMILTON, Sir WILLIAM, was granted 2000 acres at Killeny and Tadane, Barony of Strabane, County Tyrone, 20 November 1629. [CPRI]

HAMILTON, WILLIAM, of Rowbane, was granted patent of denization on 5 July 1631. [CPRI]

HAMILTON, WILLIAM, of Belymulin, born 1657, died 28 February 1720. [Old Abbey Church gravestone, Bangor, County Down]

HAMILTON, WILLIAM, in the townlands of Bright, County Down, 1659. [C]

HAMILTON, WILLIAM, in Fanagrain, parish of Devonish, County Fermanagh, 1659. [C]

HAMILTON, WILLIAM, a gentleman in Rowbane, parish of Ballyhalber, Barony of The Ards, County Down, in 1659. [C]

HAMILTON, WILLIAM, tenant of the Fisher's Quarter and of Ballygraffin, County Down, in 1681. [HM]

HAMILTON, WILLIAM, in Ballyknockan Mill, County Down, 1681. [HM]

HAMILTON, WILLIAM, tenant in Ravennas, County Down, 1681. [HM]

HAMILTON, WILLIAM, in Bangor, County Down, 1681. [HM]

HAMILTON, WILLIAM, a tenant in Ballyoran, County Down, 1681. [HM]

HAMILTON, WILLIAM, a tenant in Lisleen, Hollywood own, County Down, in 1681. [HM]

HAMILTON, WILLIAM, tenant of Strantown, Hollywood, County Down, in 1681. [HM]

HAMILTON, WILLIAM, in Knockcolumkill, County Down, in 1681. [HM]

HAMILTON, …….., a widow, a tenant in Bangor town, County Down, 1681. [HM]

HANNAH, PATRICK, a tenant in Bangor town, County Down, in 1681. [HM]

HANNAY, PATRICK, was appointed clerk to the Privy Council of Ireland on 28 May 1625. [CPRI]

HANNAY, Sir ROBERT, was appointed to the office of Clerk of the Nihils of the Court of the Exchequer on 11 December 1631. [CPRI]

HARRINGTON, THOMAS, a tenant in Munlagan, County Down, 1681. [HM]

HARRIS, JOHN, a tenant in Bangor town, County Down, 1681. [HM]

HATHORNE, ..., a widow, a tenant in Hollywood Town, County Down, in 1681. [HM]

HAY, HENRY, a Captain in Colonel Stanley's regiment in Ireland, husband of Margaret Hay, parents of Margaret Hay, a deed, 1715. [NRS.RD4.116.455]

HEIGATE, JAMES, was granted 400 acres to be known as the Manor of Heigate, in the Barony of Clankelly, County Fermanagh, on 26 August 1629. [CPRI]

HENDERSON, JOHN, born 1684, died 30 April 1740, husband of Mary Henderson. [Blaris gravestone, County Down]

HENDERSON, JOHN, a tenant in Bangor town, County Down, in 1681. [HM]

HENRY, JAMES BLACK, in Lislagan, Ballymoney, 1720. [UJA.VII.10]

HENRY, JAMES, in the Barony of Kilconway, 1720. [UJA.VII.11]

HENRY, ROBERT, a minister at Carrickfergus, a letter, 29 June 1648. [NRS.GD206.2.13]

HEPBURN, WILLIAM, in Bishop's Gate, Londonderry, 1659. [C]

HERON, JOHN, a gentleman, with 2000 acres in the precinct of Oneylan, County Armagh, 1611. [Carew mss.1611.130]

HERON, NINIAN, a gentleman, was granted land in County West Meath, 9 March 1626. [CPRI]

HILLHOUSE, ABRAHAM, a merchant in Ardkillie, County Londonderry, sold a tenement in Irvine, Ayrshire, to Robert Francis a burgess of Irvine on 17 November 1675, document written by Arthur Hamilton a notary. [NRS.GD3.871]

HODGE, DAVID, was pardoned for the murder of Sir John Wemyss, 6 May 1629. [CPRI]

HOGG, WILLIAM, a tenant in Ballyskelly and Ballow near Bangor, County Down, in 1681. [HM]

HOGG, WILLIAM, a tenant in Ringneale, Manor of Ballydeine, County Down, 1681. [HM]

HOGGE, WILLIAM, of Rathgil, born 1645, died 29 September 1704. [Old Abbey Church gravestone, Bangor, County Down]

HOLLYDAY, WILLIAM, a tenant in Bangor town, County Down, 1681. [HM]

HOMILL, MATHEW, a burgess of Irvine, 'now in Dunbug in Ireland', a creditor of Jean Campbell, spouse of William

Dunlop of Craig in Kilmaurs, Ayrshire, testament, confirmed 1621, Comm. Glasgow. [NRS]

HONEYMAN, ALEXANDER, a merchant in Carrick, Ireland, was admitted as a burgess and guilds-brother of Glasgow in 1716. [GBR]

HOPE, ALEXANDER, a gentleman in Ballyfiny, Barony of Ballintobber, County Roscommon, 1659. [C]

HOUSTON, JOHN OGE, was pardoned of the alienation of lands in County Antrim to Randal, Earl of Antrim, 27 June 1631. [CPRI]

HOUSTON, ROBERT, a gentleman in Silver Street, Londonderry, 1659. [C]

HOUSTON, WILLIAM, was pardoned of the alienation of lands in County Antrim to Randal, Earl of Antrim, 27 June 1631. [CPRI]

HOUSTON, RICHARD, a gentleman in the townlands of Granfield, County Down, 1659. [C]

HOUSTON, WILLIAM, in Maddebainey, Liberty of Coleraine, 1720. [UJA.VII.10]

HOW, JOHN, in Wellbrook, County Tyrone, 1689. [NRS.GD26.8.15]

HOWATSON, MOSES, a gentleman of Belaghstoun, County Kildare, a deed, 1715. [NRS.RD2.104.1006]

HUBLETHORNE, CHARLES, son of Colonel John Hublethorne the governor of Waterford in Ireland, a deed, 1700. [NRS.RD2.83.981]

HUME, Sir JOHN, in Koltos, Parish of Devonish, County Fermanagh, 1659. [C]

HUME, PATRICK, in Devonish, County Fermanagh, 1659. [C]

HUNTER, ANDREW, in Corstoun Kill, Liberty of Coleraine, 1720. [UJA.VII.10]

HUTCHISON, ALEXANDER, a tenant in Drumneligg, County Down, 1681. [HM]

HUTCHESON, ALEXANDER, in Drumalig, parish of Tonaghneeve, County Down, will refers to his only son John Hutcheson, his grandsons Francis, Robert, and John; also his other grandsons William Wallace son of his daughter Beatrix Wallace, and John Young son of his daughter Mary Young; witnesses Hugh Fisher formerly in Edenberry parish, County Armagh, later in South Carolina, Thomas McCounchy in Ballybrawley, County Armagh, Thomas Dobbin late of Trinascobe, County Armagh, William Bruce, and Thomas Drennan, probate 26 January 1725. [DRD]

HUTCHESON, JOHN, in Ballyrea, County Armagh, will refers to his wife Rachell, his children Hans, Francis, Robert, Alexander, Rhoda, his brother in law James Johnston; witnesses Alexander Johnston, James Johnston, Thomas Drennan, James Meares in Dublin, probate 9 August 1729. [DRD]

INGLIS, JOHN, son of the late David Inglis of Claddieford, Ireland, was apprenticed to Sir James Murray of Deuchar, a merchant in Edinburgh on 26 May 1647. [Edinburgh Register of Apprentices]

INNES, ALEXANDER, son of Gilbert Innes a fermourer in

County Armagh, was apprenticed to David Gray a hat-maker in Edinburgh on 1 June 1687. [Edinburgh Register of Apprentices]

IRVINE, CHRISTOPHER, of Castle Irvine in Ireland, heir to his cousin Dr Christopher Irvine of Castle Irvine in 1714. [NRS.S/H]

IRVING, ALEXANDER, a plumber in Dublin, will refers to William Burne and Joseph Love, both gentlemen in Dublin, witnesses John Nash a distiller in Dublin, Edward Doyle a plumber in Dublin, John Connell a gentleman in Dublin, and James Rose, probate3 September 1715. [DRD]

IRVING, CHRISTOPHER, heir to his father Thomas Irving a surgeon apothecary in Dublin, 1713. [NRS.S/H]

IRVING, EDWARD, a gentleman in Lagbane, Barony of Tireagh, County Sligo, 1659. [C]

IRVING, JOHN, a gentleman in Templeboy, Barony of Tireagh, County Sligo, 1659. [C]

IRVING, THOMAS, heir to his brother Christopher Irving, son of Thomas Irving a surgeon in Dublin, 1715. [NRS.S/H]

IRVING, THOMAS, of Dumcoltran, son of the late Thomas Irving a surgeon apothecary in Dublin, testaments, 1728, 1733, Comm. Dumfries. [NRS]

IRVING, Sir WILLIAM, with 1500 acres in County Leitrim, 25 May 1625. [CPRI]

IRVING, WILLIAM, of Bonshaw in Annandale, an attorney in Belfast, 1651. [TBB]

IRWIN, JOHN, a gentleman in Carowmabine, Barony of Tireragh, County Sligo, 1659. [C]

IRWIN, WILLIAM, a gentleman in Ballenadolagh, parish of Derryvolan, County Fermanagh, 1659. [C]

JACKSON, JAMES, in Newtown, County Down, will refers to his brother John Jackson of Ballygregin and his son James and Gilbert son of John Jackson of Ballyskeagh, to nephew John Teat, James Neill tenant in Ballymasea, John Thompson and John Jackson both in Newtown, Elizabeth Cord, servants James Sloane and Martha Wither; witnesses Thomas Jackson innkeeper in Newtown, John Thomson a merchant in Newtown, John Mair minister in Newtown, and James Orr, probate 18 February 1712. [DRD]

JACKSON, JOHN, tenant in the Church Quarter of Dundonell, County Down, in 1681. [HM]

JAMIESON, WILLIAM, in town of Letterkenny, parish of Cornwall, Barony of Killmccrenan, County Donegal, 1659. [C]

JOHNSTON, ANDREW, agent for Sir Andrew MacLellan, residing in the Precinct of Boylagh in 1611. [Carew.Mss.58]

JOHNSTON, Cornet ARCHIBALD, a descendant of the Johnston of Loderhay family in Annandale, died in March 167-, husband of Margaret Graham. [Castlederg Church of Ireland gravestone, County Tyrone]

JOHNSTON, DAVID, in Donagh parish, County Monaghan, in 1659. [C]

JOHNSTON, DAVID, a gentleman in Tullikelher, parish of Devonish, County Fermanagh, 1659. [C]

JOHNSTON, JOHN, a gentleman in Tullikelher, parish of Devonish, County Fermanagh, 1659. [C]

JOHNSTON, JOHN, a gentleman in Tullicolerick, parish of Magherycoolemoney, County Fermanagh, 1659. [C]

JOHNSTON, JOHN, a tenant in Ballywaltertown, County Down, 1681. [HM]

JOHNSTON, Ensign ROBERT, a gentleman in Kilordrunly, County Fermanagh, 1659. [C]

JOHNSTON, SYMON, in the Barony of Magheryboy, County Fermanagh, 1631. [PRONI.T.934]

JOHNSTON, WALTER, a gentleman in the townlands of Rademane, County Down, 1659. [C]

JOHNSTON, WALTER, a gentleman in Lawry, parish of Templecarne, County Fermanagh, 1659. [C]

JOHNSTON, WILLIAM, in the Barony of Magheryboy, County Fermanagh, 1631. [PRONI.T.934]

JOHNSTON, WILLIAM, jr., in the Barony of Magheryboy, County Fermanagh, 1631. [PRONI.T.934]

JOHNSTON, WILLIAM, a gentleman in Donagh parish, County Monaghan, in 1659. [C]

JOLLIE, PETER, in Drumnakill, Barony of Carey. 1720. [UJA.VII.11]

KELLY, EDMOND, a tenant in Bangor town, County Down, 1681. [HM]

KELLY, JAMES, a tenant in Bangor town, County Down, in 1681. [HM]

KENDALL, EDWARD, in Dublin, 1637, letters. [NRS.GD406.1.381/383]

KENNEDY, ALEXANDER, born in Belfast, County Antrim, took the Oath of Allegiance and Supremacy to King Charles II, on 7 November 1672.

KENNEDY, A., in Dublin, 1689. [NRS.GD406.1.3511]

KENNEDY, ANTHONY, of Balsarach, died 3 December 1620. [Derrykeighan gravestone, County Antrim]

KENNEDY, ANTHONY, in Moncloyt, parish of Ray, Barony of Raphoe, County Donegal, 1659. [C]

KENNEDY, ALEXANDER, a merchant in Newry, County Down, a deed, 1702. [NRS.RD2.86.1.372]

KENNEDY, ALEXANDER, a merchant in Rathfriland, Ireland, a deed, 1702. [NRS.RD2.86.1.64]

KENNEDY, DANIEL, in Ballyskeagh, Barony of the Ards, County Down, 1659. [C]

KENNEDY, DAVID, tenant of Ballyrobert, Ballydavy, Cragivad, and Ballygreny, County Down, in 1681. [HM]

KENNEDY, FERGUS, in the townlands of Ballyloghan, County Down, 1659. [C]

KENNEDY, GEORGE, a tenant in Bangor town, County Down, in 1681. [HM]

KENNEDY, Dr HUGH, tenant of Carrocreagh, County Down, in 1681. [HM]

KENNEDY, JAMES, a tenant in Bangor town, County Down, 1681. [HM]

KENNEDY, JOHN, a tenant in Hollywood Town, County Down, in 1681. [HM]

KENNEDY, MARJORIE, daughter of Thomas Kennedy of Balltersan, and spouse of James Hamilton, son of James Hamilton of Derrybuy in Ireland, a deed, 1700. [NRS.RD2.83.721]

KENNEDY, OLIVER, was granted patent of denization on 5 July 1631. [CPRI]

KENNEDY, THOMAS, a gentleman in High Street, Dublin, in 1659. [C]

KENNEDY, WILLIAM, a gentleman in Lenthrops Alley, Dublin, in 1659. [C]

KERR, DAVID, in Gelagh, Liberty of Coleraine, 1720. [UJA.VII.10]

KERR, ROBERT, died 7 November 1676, and Sara Kerr, died 2 November 1714. [Derryveighen gravestone, County Antrim]

KERR, ROBERT, in Cappagh, Liberty of Coleraine, 1720. [UJA.VII.10]

KNIGHT, JANET, in Glasgow, testament, 8 January 1652, Comm. Glasgow, [NRS]; daughter of the late Alexander Knight in Ballachry near Coleraine in the Kingdom of Ireland,

KNOX, ALEXANDER, a gentleman in Killigadan, parish of Donoghmore, Barony of Raphoe, County Donegal, 1659. [C]

KNOX, GEORGE, a gentleman in the parish of Drumhome, Barony of Tirhugh, County Donegal, 1659. [C]

KNOX, JAMES, in Killmore, parish of Gartan, Barony of Killmccrenan, County Donegal, 1659. [C]

KNOX, SYMON, master of the Thomas and Ralph of Dublin, captured by Parliamentary forces when bound from Dublin to Liverpool in 1644. [TNA.HCA.13.59.518]

KNOX, THOMAS, in Dungannon, County Tyrone, Member of the Irish Parliament for the borough of Newton Ards in 1692. [MM]

KNOX, THOMAS, of Lough Easke, County Donegal, will refers to his cousin Lettice Knox, his sister Lettice Knox or Short, sister Elizabeth Short of Parke, Thomas Young, son of sister Katherine Knox, cousin Mrs Richard Mansfield and her children including sons Ralph and Francis, uncle Patrick Hamilton and his son George, Charles Knox natural son of brother Charles, cousin Ralph, Francis and Charles Mansfeld, cousin William Hamilton of Killeter, cousin James Hamilton of Lough McHall, and his nephew Archibald Hamilton, cousin Jenny Dixon and her sister Lettice, Thomas Knox son of George Knox, George Knox and his brother Andrew, Captain James Hamilton of Brownhall and his brother Abraham, Mr Hamilton of Ballinfatter, Major Guy Carleton, his brother Christopher Hamilton and sister Irwin Carleton, Alexander Murray of Broughton, William Conyngham, Creighton Young, Alexander Nesbit an attorney, Mr Wybrants, Dr Hamilton, Captain John McCausland, Oliver Nugent, …Macky, Miss Ferguson, Moses Thompson, McGowan and McGowan, Thomas Brown and sister Jenny, Rebecca Knox and James Brown, James Wilson servant, Ralph Gore, John Young, Reverend Dr Andrew Hamilton, Oliver McCausland, , Alexander Nesbitt; witnesses Robert Bustard, Henry Gorell and James Woodward yeomen in Lougheask, County Donegal, Isaac Walsh, Robert Wallis NP, Probate, 1 July 1721. [DRD]

KNOX, THOMAS, in Dungannon, will refers to Colonel Edward Bryce in Belfast his brother-in-law, Arthur Knox of Tweebeg, County Mayo, his son in law Charles Echlin and his wife Ann Knox, his nephew Thomas Knox; witnesses John Brown, George Lamie and John Jordan all gentlemen in Dungannon, Edward Jones a clerk to Edward Mathews a gentleman in Dublin, probate 25 July 1728. [DRD]

KNOX, Major, in Ray, parish of Auchnish, Barony of Killmccrenan, County Donegal, 1659. [C]

KYLE, HUGH, a merchant in Dublin, will refers to his wife Margery, their children Samuel and Hannah; witnesses John Warren a servant, William Souch a clerk to William Barry in Dublin, and said William Barry a scrivener, probate 4 July 1723. [DRD]

LACKEY, JANE, born 1681, from Carrickfergus, a servant indented for 5 years, emigrated via Liverpool aboard the Experiment of Liverpool, master Cavaleiro Christian, bound for Pennsylvania, Virginia or Maryland in August 1699. [LRO]

 LANG, JOHN, a tenant in Hollywood Town, County Down, in 1681. [HM]

LAUGHLIN, ..., a widow, a tenant in Hollywood Town, County Down, in 1681. [HM]

LAUDER, ALEXANDER, resident agent to William Lauder in the Precinct of Fewes in 1611. [Carew.Mss.58]

LAUDER, GEORGE, deputy to Sir James Douglas in the Precinct of Fewes in 1611. [Carew.Mss.58]

LAUDERDALE, ROBERT, a gentleman in Ardvenehan, parish of Devonish, County Fermanagh, 1659. [C]

LAWSON, WILLIAM, a gentleman in Kilkighan, Barony of Boylagh and Banagh, County Donegal, 1659. [C]

LEAD, ..., the widow, a tenant in Ballywaltertown, County Down, in 1681. [HM]

LECKIE, ALEXANDER, a merchant in Londonderry, was permitted to send provisions to Londonderry aboard the Prosperity of Glasgow, master William Adair, in 1689. [RPCS.XIII.555]

LECKY, JAMES, in Leck, parish of Leck, Barony of Raphoe, County Donegal, 1659. [C]

LECKY, JOHN, a burgess of Johnstown, 3 April 1627. [CPRI]

LECKY, WALTER, was granted 600 acres in County Longford, 28 May 1625; a burgess of Johnstown, was granted 3366 acres in County Longford to be called the Manor of Eden, 3 April 1627. [CPRI]

LENNOX, ARCHIBALD, a tenant in Hollywood Town, County Down, in 1681. [HM]

LENNOX, JAMES, Duke of, was granted lands in the Barony of Raphoe, County Donegal, to be called the Manor of Lismolmoghery, 24 January 1629. [CPRI]

LENNOX, JAMES, a merchant in Silver Street, Londonderry, 1659. [C]

LENNOX, JOHN, vicar of Trevet, County Meath, 18 January 1631. [CPRI]

LENNOX, ALEXANDER, a merchant in Londonderry, was permitted to send provisions to Londonderry aboard the

Prosperity of Glasgow, master William Adair, in 1689.
[RPCS.XIII.555]

LENNOX, ROBERT, born 1661, a merchant in Belfast, died
17 February 1733, husband of [1] Ann Drennan Lecky, [2] Ann
Conyngham, [3] Martha, daughter of John Hamilton sovereign
of Belfast. [Old Poorhouse gravestone, Belfast]

LENNOX, WILLIAM, a gentleman, in Ray, parish of Ray,
Barony of Raphoe, County Donegal, 1659. [C]

LENNOX, ..., a widow, a tenant in Bangor town, County
Down, in 1681. [HM]

LESLEY, HENRY, was appointed Dean of Down, 30 March
1627. [CPRI]

LESLEY, JAMES, in the townlands of Sheepland begg and
Newtown, County Down, 1659. [C]

LESLEY, JOHN, a merchant in Coleraine, bound from
Holland to Scotland, was captured at sea by a French privateer
in 1710. [NRS.AC10.100]

LESLIE, JOHN, Dean of Dromore, "to be buried in the
ancient burying place of my ancestors in the parish church of
Donagh in the town of Castle Leslie", will refers to his wife
Elizabeh, nephew Henry Leslie, nephew Robert Leslie, niece
Jane Leslie, Michael Ward in Dublin, Charles Campbell in
Dublin, David Wilson in Dublin; witnesses Reverend William
Hamilton Archdeacon of Armagh, John Pringle gentleman of
Callidon, County Tyrone, Samuel Black a gentleman of Creegy,
County Monaghan, Robert Lowry jr.a gentleman in Aghenis,
County Monaghan, probate 6 November 1722. [DRD]

LEVINGSTON, SAMUEL, was granted a pass to go to Ireland 16 May 1656. [CalSPDom.1655.582]

LINDSEY, ANDREW, in Drumenan, County Donegal, will refers to his wife Margaret, his daughter Susanna and her husband Robert Patterson; witnesses John Lindsey, John Cadow in Tullyowen, County Donegal, Henry Solesberry a shoemaker in Maymore, County Donegal, John McClintock, and George Luke, probate 14 November 1715. [DRD]

LINDSAY, JAMES, a gentleman in Drumenan, parish of Taghboine, County Donegal, 1659. [C]

LINDSAY, JAMES, a tenant in Bangor town, County Down, in 1681. [HM]

LINDSAY, JOHN, a tenant in Bangor town, County Down, 1681. [HM]

LINDSAY, MATTHEW, a gentleman in Maymore, parish of Taghboine, County Donegal, 1659. [C]

LINDSAY, ROBERT, a gentleman, was granted land in County West Meath, on 9 March 1626. [CPRI]

LINDSAY, ROBERT, a tenant in Bangor town, County Down, in 1681. [HM]

LINDSAY, THOMAS, a gentleman in the townlands of Clogher, County Down, 1659. [C]

LITTLE, ARCHIBALD, in the Barony of Magheryboy, County Fermanagh, 1631. [PRONI.T.934]

LITTLE, JOHN, in the Barony of Magheryboy, County Fermanagh, 1631. [PRONI.T.934]

LOCH, JAMES, a yeoman in County Cork, 'a tory, thief or

robber', to be apprehended and tried, 1692.
[HMC.Ormonde.ii.449]

LOCKART, RICHARD, a tenant in Ballywaltertown, County Down, 1681. [HM]

LOGAN, JOHN, a tenant in Bangor town, County Down, in 1681. [HM]

LOGAN, ROBERT, a tenant in Bangor town, County Down, in 1681. [HM]

LOGAN, ..., a widow, a tenant in Bangor town, County Down, 1681. [HM]

LONG, ROBERT, a tenant in Ballywaltertown, County Down, 1681. [HM]

LOTHIAN, JOHN, sometime minister at Dundonald in Ireland, thereafter at Monkland in Scotland, now in Ireland, husband of Agnes Neish in Monkland, her testament, 1658, Comm. Glasgow. [NRS]

LOWDON, ..., a widow, a tenant in Hollywood Town, County Down, in 1681. [HM]

LOWRY, ALEXANDER, a gentleman in Lesaghnegrogh, parish of Drumully, County Fermanagh, 1659. [C]

LUGTON, GEORGE, sometime in Urquhat, bound for Ireland, 21 May 1613. [Dunfermline Burgh Records]

LUKE, JOHN, a tenant in Bangor town, County Down, 1681. [HM]

LUNDY, JAMES, tenant in the Church Quarter of Dundonell, County Down, in 1681. [HM]

LUTHERSDALE, JAMES, a tenant in Ballywaltertown, County Down, 1681. [HM]

LYN, WILLIAM, in Raphoe, County Donegal, 23 November 1665. [NRS.GD1.693.13]

LYNDSEY, JAMES, born in Londonderry, a merchant, took the Oath of Allegiance and Supremacy to King Charles II, on 13 April 1670.

MCALPINE, ALEXANDER, in Monaghan, Ireland, was admitted as a burgess and guilds-brother of Glasgow in 1718. [GBR]

MCAMT, ALEXANDER, a tenant in Bangor town, County Down, in 1681. [HM]

MCARTHUR, Reverend JOHN, born 1651, died 27 February 1716, and his wife Margaret Ross, born 1686, died 16 October 1761, parents of Reverend Dennis McArthur, born 1714, died 11 January 1796, and Elisabeth McArthur, born 1719, died 15 February 1796. [Layde, Cushendall gravestone, County Antrim]

MACAULAY, ALEXANDER, in Drumnagee, Barony of Carey. 1720. [UJA.VII.11]

MCAUSLAN, ALEXANDER, in Whitehead, County Antrim, a deed, 1714. [NRS.RD2.104.297]

MCBRIDE, JAMES, born 1712, died 7 May 1772. [Dromara gravestone, County Down]

MCBRIDE, JOHN, born 1729, died 29 April 1800. [Dromara gravestone, County Down]

MACCABE, DUGALL, was pardoned for the murder of Sir John Wemyss, on 6 May 1629. [CPRI]

MCCALDEN, ANDREW, a tenant in Bangor town, County Down, in 1681. [HM]

MCCALL, JOHN, in Kurgan, a letter, 7 December 1713. [TCD.750.1475]

MCCARDY, JOHN, a tenant in Bangor town, County Down, in 1681. [HM]

MCCARLY, JAMES, a tenant in Bangor town, County Down, in 1681. [HM]

MCCARLY, THOMAS, a tenant in Bangor town, County Down, in 1681. [HM]

MCCARLY, ..., a widow, a tenant in Bangor town, County Down, in 1681. [HM]

MCCARTNEY, ALEXANDER, a tenant in Bangor town, County Down, in 1681. [HM]

MCCAUSLAND, Captain CHARLES, in Omagh, County Tyrone, a letter, 25 July 1801. [TCD.750.819]

MCCLAINE, Reverend JOHN, in Coleraine, a letter, 29 May 1694; inducted to Antrim and Templepark in May 1700. [TCD.750.358/1693]

MCCLELLAND, ADAM, a gentleman in Crafford, parish of Clandevadock, Barony of Killmccrenan, County Donegal, 1659. [C]

MCCLURGH, WILLIAM, a tenant in Ballywaltertown, County Down, in 1681. [HM]

MCCLUIR, ANDREW, in Ireland, a creditor of Jean Campbell, spouse of William Dunlop of Craig in Kilmaurs,

Ayrshire, testament, 1621, Comm. Glasgow. [NRS]

MACCOLLUM, ALEXANDER, in Lignamanoge, in the Barony of Kilconway, 1720. [UJA.VII.11]

MACCOLLUM, JAMES, in Carnanrigg, Liberty of Coleraine, 1720. [UJA.VII.10]

MCCOLMAN, ARCHIBALD, in Park, Barony of Dunluce, 1720. [UJA.VII.9]

MCCOMB, ..., wife of John McComb, born 1701, died 13 February 1737. [Donaghcloney gravestone, County Down]

MCCOMBE, WILLIAM, a tenant in Bangor town, County Down, 1681. [HM]

MCCONNELL, CAUGHTRY, a tenant in Bangor town, County Down, in 1681. [HM]

MCCONNELL, JAMES, born in 1596 in Groomsport, County Down, a mariner aboard the Katherine of Groomsport, a witness before the High Court of the Admiralty of England in May 1639. [TNA.HCA.13.55.43]

MCCORMICK, WILLIAM, a tenant in Bangor town, County Down, in 1681. [HM]

MCCREA, MATTHEW, a tenant in Ballywaltertown, County Down, in 1681. [HM]

MCCREERY, ROBERT, a tenant in Ballow near Bangor, County Down, in 1681. [HM]

MCCREERY, ROBERT, in Bangor, County Down, 1681. [HM]

MCCUBBIN, KATHERINE, in the parish of Colmonell, Ayrshire, Scotland, testament, 4 June 1698, Comm. Glasgow, [NRS], daughter of the late John McCubbin in 'Dinnie-may' in the Kingdom of Ireland.

MCCULLEN, THOMAS, a tenant in Ballywaltertown, County Down, in 1681. [HM]

MCCULLOCH, ALEXANDER, of Ballycopeland, County Down, bound for America in 1718. [NRS.GD10.1421,.1/46]

MCCUTCHION, ADAM, a merchant in Belfast, will refers to his children Isabel, Margaret, Thomas and Jane, his brother James, his brother Robert's children, his sister and her son Archibald, his brother in law Archibald Craig, his brother in law Robert Allen, Joseph Innis and William Stevenson; witnesses Reverend Samuel Ross in Londonderry, James White a cooper in Belfast, John Hamilton apprentice to William Stevenson, Robert Armstrong, John Johnston and his wife Jane Johnston, probate 3 January 1718. [DRD]

MCDONNELL, RANDOLPH, Earl of Antrim, died 1621.? [Bun-na-margie Friary gravestone, County Antrim]

MCDONNELL, RANDLE, Lord Marquis of Antrim, born 9 June 1610, died 3 February 1682. [Bun-na-margie Friary gravestone, County Antrim]

MCDONNELL, RANDLE WILLIAM, Marquis of Antrim, born 4 November 1719, died 28 July 1791. [Bun-na-margie Friary gravestone, County Antrim]

MCDONNELL, ALEXANDER, Earl of Antrim, born 1713, died 1775. [Bun-na-margie Friary gravestone, County Antrim]

MCDONNELL, ANN, Countess of Antrim, born 1716, died 14

January 1753. [Bun-na-margie Friary gravestone, County Antrim]

MCDONNELL, Captain ARCHIBALD, born 1647, son of Major General Alexander McDonnell, died 28 December 1720, also his wife Ann Stewart, born 1646, died 6 April 1714, and their son Coll McDonnell, born 1688, died 6 June 1737. [Layde, Cushendall gravestone, County Antrim]

MCDONNELL, COLL, of Kilmore, son of Major General Sir Alexander McDonnell and his wife daughter of McAlister of Loup, died 25 March 1719. [Layde, Cushendall gravestone, County Antrim]

MCDONNELL, JOHN, in Ballylig, in the Barony of Kilconway, 1720. [UJA.VII.11]

MCDONNELL, JOHN, in Coolnagappage, Barony of Carey. 1720. [UJA.VII.11]

MCDONNELL, MCCOLL, of Kilmore, born 1645, died 23 March 1719. [Layde, Cushendall gravestone, County Antrim]

MCDOWELL, ALEXANDER, in the townlands of Ballebeane, County Down, 1659. [C]

MCDOWELL, BENJAMIN, a linen-draper in Rathmore, parish of Dunegar, County Antrim, will refers to his children Elizabeth, Anne, John, and Benjamin, Thomas Banks a gentleman in Belfast, John Allen a linen draper in Drumnadarragh, George McMaster a gentleman in Antrim, County Antrim; witnesses William Rodger a linen draper in Rathmore, Robert Carswell a linen draper in Rathmore, William Boyd a farmer in Dunegar, probate 26 June 1728. [DRD]

MCDOWELL, JAMES, a tenant in Bangor town, County Down, in 1681. [HM]

MCDOWELL, JOHN, a tenant in Hollywood Town, County Down, in 1681. [HM]

MCDOWELL, JOHN, in the parish of Mullaghbrack, County Armagh, will refers to his sons Daniel and John, grandson William McDowell, Hugh Grier's children, John Scott son of Quintin Scott, all of Derrynaght, County Armagh; witnesses John Brennand in Armagh, and Deb. Brennand, probate 22 June 1719. [DRD]

MCDOWELL, MARY, wife of John McCulloch in Ireland, was served heir to her grand-father Uthred McDowell of Barjarge in Carrick on 25 October 1636. [NRS.Retours.Ayr.316]

MCDOWELL, PATRICK, a tenant in Bangor town, County Down, in 1681. [HM]

MCFALL, GILL., in Lislagan, Ballymoney, 1720. [UJA.VII.10]

MCFERRAN, THOMAS, a tenant in Bangor town, County Down, in 1681. [HM]

MCGIBBON, ARCHIBALD, a tenant in Bangor town, County Down, in 1681. [HM]

MCGILL, HUGH, a gentleman in Ballyhonney, parish of Newton, Barony of the Ards, County Down, 1659. [C]

MAGILL, HUGH, of Kirkstoun, County Down, a lease, 1687. [PRONI.D24]

MAGILL, Sir JOHN, of Gillhall, County Down, a lease, 1687. [PRONI.D24]

MCGUIRE, Reverend JACKSON, tenant in the Church Quarter of Dundonell, County Down, in 1681. [HM]

MCHAILL, JOHN, a tenant in Hollywood Town, County Down, in 1681. [HM]

MCHAILE, JOHN, a tenant in Bangor town, County Down, in 1681. [HM]

MCILWRAITH, THOMAS, a tenant in Ballygranny, County Down, 1681. [HM]

MACHENRY, JAMES, in Ballumacaldrick, in the Barony of Kilconway, 1720. [UJA.VII.11]

MCKAY, DANIEL, born 1716, died 2 April 1736. [Bun-na-margie Friary gravestone, County Antrim]

MCKEE, JOHN, a tenant in Bangor town, County Down, 1681. [HM]

MCKELVEY, NINIAN, a tenant in Bangor town, County Down, in 1681. [HM]

MCKELVEY, NINIAN, a tenant in Bangor town, County Down, in 1681. [HM]

MCKELVEY, ..., a widow, a tenant in Bangor town, County Down, 1681. [HM]

MACKESON, GEORGE, Dean of Armagh, 12 May 1627. [CPRI]

MACKILLWIE, JOHN, in Ireland, a bond, 24 October 1661. [NRS.RD2.2.811]

MCKINNEY, ALEXANDER, a merchant in Nevis and St Kitts in 1661, agent for George McCartney a merchant in Belfast. [PRONI.MCI19.1]

MCLAUGHLIN, JOHN, a tenant in Hollywood Town, County Down, in 1681. [HM]

MCLEAGH, JOHN, of Cloughhcorr, Barony of Dunluce, 1720. [UJA.VII.9]

MCLELLAN, Sir ROBERT, was granted land in West Meath, 7 October 1629. [CPRI]

MACLELLAN, ROBERT, of Bellynashie, born 1684, died 19 August 1751, husband of [1] Margaret McAlexander, born 1683, died 5 January 1741. [Rasbee gravestone, County Antrim]

MCLOUGHLIN, JAMES, in Lignamanoge, in the Barony of Kilconway, 1720. [UJA.VII.11]

MCMICHAEL, MARY, died 4 August 1714. [Bun-na-margie Friary gravestone, County Antrim]

MCMICHAN, JOHN, a tenant in Bangor town, County Down, 1681. [HM]

MCMICHAN, ALICE, a tenant in Ballynegee near Bangor, County Down, in 1681. [HM]

MCMICHAN, JAMES, a tenant in Bangor town, County Down, in 1681. [HM]

MCMICHAN, JOHN, a shoemaker, a tenant in Bangor town, County Down, in 1681. [HM]

MCMICHAN, JOHN, master of the <u>Janet of Belfast</u> at Findhorn, Morayshire, bound for Dieppe, France, with a cargo of salmon and herring, 1717. ['Social Life in former days', Edinburgh, 1865]

MCMICHAN, PATRICK, a tenant in Bangor town, County Down, in 1681. [HM]

MCMICHAN, WILLIAM, a tenant in Bangor town, County Down, in 1681. [HM]

MCMICHAN, ..., a widow, a tenant in Bangor town, County Down, in 1681. [HM]

MCMORLAN, WILLIAM, a tenant in Ballywaltertown, County Down, in 1681. [HM]

MCMULLEN, HUGH, a tenant in Hollywood Town, County Down, in 1681. [HM]

MCMULLEN, ENEAS, a tenant in Ballywaltertown, County Down, in 1681. [HM]

MCMURRAY, JAMES, a tenant in Hollywood Town, County Down, in 1681. [HM]

MCNARTY, JOHN, a tenant in Ballywaltertown, County Down, **1681.** [HM]

MCNAGHTEN, FRANCIS, a salmon fisher in Portneen, Barony of Dunluce, 1720. [UJA.VII.9]

MCNAUGHTON, JOHN, First secretary to the first Earl of

Antrim, died 1630. [Bun-na-margie Friary gravestone, County Antrim]

MCNAGHTEN, THOMAS, in Gallanagh, in the Barony of Kilconway, 1720. [UJA.VII.11]

MCNEALE, ROBERT, was appointed vicar of Emgall and Killeed in the diocese of Down on 6 June 1631. [CPRI]

MCNEIL, Reverend ARCHIBALD, in Billy, a letter, 22 October 1700, [TCD.750.731]; in Derryveighen, 1714. [Derryveighen gravestone, County Antrim]

MCNEILY, JOHN, tenant in the Church Quarter of Dundonell, County Down, in 1681. [HM]

MCNILY, JAMES, a tenant in Bangor town, County Down, in 1681. [HM]

MCPHERSON, ANDREW, a tenant in Bangor town, County Down, in 1681. [HM]

MCROBINS, ALEXANDER, a tenant in Ballywaltertown, County Down, 1681. [HM]

MALCOLM, J., in Dunmurray, a letter, 29 August 1710. [TCD.750.1381]

MALLY, GEORGE, a tenant in Hollywood Town, County Down, in 1681. [HM]

MANFOD, HUGH, born 1676, died 15 October 1751, husband of Elizabeth Snoddy, died 12 August 1726. [Larne gravestone, County Antrim]

MARSHALL, GEAN, born 1706, died 22 July 1781. [Dromara gravestone, County Down]

MARSHALL, JOHN MATTHEW, a tenant in McBride's Quarter, Manor of Ballydeine, County Down, 1681. [HM]

MARSHALL, MATTHEW, a tenant in McBride's Quarter, Manor of Ballydeine, County Down, 1681. [HM]

MARTIN, Mrs DOROTHY, a widow late of Dublin, a decree in Edinburgh, 6 June 1728. [ECA.MB.VI.159/6067]

MARTIN, FINLAY, a tenant in Bangor town, County Down, in 1681. [HM]

MARTIN, GEORGE, born 1617, a merchant from Carrickfergus, County Antrim, 1644. [TNA.HCA.13.59.209; 59.191]

MARTIN, JAMES, died in January 1709. [Templepatrick gravestone, County Antrim]

MARTIN, WILLIAM, a tenant in Bangor town, County Down, 1681. [HM]

MAULE, THOMAS, was granted denization and appointed joint Surveyor General of Customs in Ireland, 13 December 1627. [CPRI]

MAULE, THOMAS, in St George's Lane, Dublin, in 1659. [C]

MAULE, WILLIAM, in Dublin, letters, 1683/1693. [NRS.GD45.14.179/192]

MAXWELL, ALEXANDER, a tenant in Bangor town, County Down, 1681. [HM]

MAXWELL, ARTHUR, in Drumbeg, County Down, will refers to his wife Anne, his sister Margaret and her husband

Archibald Hamilton, their sons James a merchant in Belfast,
Arthur a merchant in Liverpool, Archibald in Rotterdam, and
daughters Mary and Ann, grand-nephew Maxwell Hamilton,
son of Arthur Hamilton in Liverpool, nieces Katherine Maxwell
or Manin, her brother James Hamilton, her husband Michael
Mankin and their son Arthur Mankin, sister in law Mrs Elinor
Stewart, and her daughter Anne Stewart, niece Anne Stewart a
widow in Newry, her children Arthur, Alexander, James and
Katherine, niece Catherine Rainey, nephew William Rainey jr a
merchant and sons Arthur, John and William, sister Elizabeth
Maxwell or Shaw, niece Mary Shaw, sister Mrs Helena Shaw or
Dalway, brother Henry Dalway, nephew Robert Dalway , his
wife and sisters Betty, Elinor and Leny Dalway, niece Jane
Maxwell or Kennedy a widow in Londonderry, brother Oliver
McCausland in Strabane and his niece Jane Kennedy in
Londonderry, Hugh Henry in Dublin, William Rainey jr, in
Belfast, Joseph Marriott in Thomas Street, Dublin, Arthur
Maxwell son of John Maxwell in Strabane, Patrick Maxwell in
Belfast, John Dalway in Dublin, Isaac McCartney, Reverend
James Kilpatrick in Belfast, James Cobham in Broad Island,
Robert Rainey in Newry, George Long in Loughbrickland,
Michael Bruce in Hollywood, Arthur Maxwell son of George
Maxwell of Dalswinton near Dumfries in Scotland, Andrew
Craford, Richard Maxwell in Strabane, James Stewart of
Kirkdonald, Alexander Tomkins in Prehenne, John Brown in
Killeleagh, Archibald Edmondstone in Duntreath, Edward
Bruce, Patrick Bruce, Reverend James Bruce, John Malcolm in
Dunmurry; witnesses William McCullogh in Ballydrain,
County Antrim, Gaven Barr farmer in Tulligowan, County
Down, James Stevenson farmer in Drumbeg, John Gowdy a
servant, David Donaldson farmer in Drumbeg, and John Ker,
probate 25 February 1721. [DRD]

MAXWELL, Dr C., in Belfast, a letter, 10 June 1712.
[TCD.750.1430]

MAXWELL, GEORGE, in Sheep Street, Dublin, in 1659. [C]

MAXWELL, HENRY, in Finneborgue, Down, a letter, 19 July 1714. [TCD.750.1498]

MAXWELL, JAMES, in Grenechoche, Ireland, a sasine, Kirkcudbright, 26 January 1623. [NRS.RS1.12.131]

MAXWELL, JAMES, in Carrickfergus, 1647. [TBB]

MAXWELL, JAMES, in the parish of Anslow, Londonderry, 1659. [C]

MAXWELL, JAMES, of Tressilly, County Down, 1663. [PRONI.T307]

MAXWELL, JAMES, a Lieutenant of the Earl of Dunbarton's Regiment which landed at Kinsale in April 1679. [HMC.Ormonde.ii.219]

MAXWELL, JAMES, tenant of Ballyharbert, Ballyharbert Mill, Balliesbrough, and Rowbane, in The Ards, County Down in 1681. [HM]

MAXWELL, JAMES, a tenant in Drumbuie, County Down, 1681. [HM]

MAXWELL, JAMES, in Pettico, Ireland, a deed, 1715. [NRS.RD4.117.876]

MAXWELL, JOHN, master of the Jonas of the Rosses, 1614. [UPB.106]

MAXWELL, Sir JOHN, commissioned to undertake the wardship of Randal McDonnell, Viscount Dunluce, 3 March 1630. [CPRI]

MAXWELL, ROBERT, was appointed rector of Tynon and

Toaghie in the Diocese of Armagh, 22 November 1625, and Archdeacon of Down Cathedral, 18 August 1628. [CPRI]

MAXWELL, Sir ROBERT, in the parish of Anslow, Londonderry, 1659. [C]

MAXWELL, ROBERT, of Ballyquintane, County Down, 1663. [PRONI.T307]

MAXWELL, ROBERT, a tenant in Granshaugh near Bangor, County Down, in 1681. [HM]

MEARNS, ROBERT, born 1668, a tanner in Larne, died 7 February 1734, husband [1] of Margaret Snoddy who died 17 November 1709, father of John Mearns who died 25 May 1717 and Thomas Mearns who died 15 July 1729. [Larne gravestone, County Antrim]

MELDRUM, JOHN, was granted the Manor of Dresternan by King James on 24 April 1617 which were later transferred to Lord James Balfour. [CSPI]

MELDRUM, Captain, agent for Lord Burleigh, in the Barony of Knockninny, County Fermanagh, with 20 men, 1611. [Carew mss.58]

MELVILLE, or MELVIN, PATRICK, a Captain of the Earl of Dunbarton's Regiment which landed at Kinsale in April 1679, later in Tymolege. [HMC.Ormonde.ii.219]

MELVIN, JAMES, a gentleman in the townlands of Clareoch, County Down, 1659. [C]

MICHELBURNE, JOHN, in Londonderry, a letter, 1689. [NRS.GD406.1.3527]

MILDMAY, DANIEL, fled from Lisburn, County Antrim, to Scotland, but returned in 1690. [RPCS.XV.25]

MILDMAY, RICHARD, of Lisburn Castle, County Antrim, fled to Scotland and died there by 1690. [RPCS.XV.25]

MILDMAY, THOMAS, fled from Lisburn, County Antrim, to Scotland, but returned in 1690. [RPCS.XV.25]

MILNE, DAVID, master of the David of Portaferry trading between Rotterdam, the Netherlands, and Dumfries, Scotland, 1722. [NRS.AC9.846]

MILTON, JOSIAS, a tenant in Hollywood Town, County Down, in 1681. [HM]

MITCHELL, JAMES, born in County Antrim 1658, brown hair, enlisted as a horseman of the King's Guard in Ireland, 1676. [HMC.Ormonde.ii.237]

MITCHELL, JAMES, a tenant in Ballywaltertown, County Down, 1681. [HM]

MITCHELL, JOHN, a gentleman in Machregorach, County Antrim, will refers to his wife, their children William, John, his brother Hugh Mitchell and his children Hugh, Elisabeth, and Rose, his brother-in-law Henry McCulloch, and his brother James Mitchell; witnesses John Brice and John McCamrick his servants, Hugh Mitchell in Glenarme, County Antrim, also Alexander Hutcheson a gentleman in Dublin, probate 19 April 1725. [DRD]

MITCHELLHILL, JOHN, minister of Ballyphilip, Ireland, son and heir of John Mitchellhill, merchant burgess of

Edinburgh, and his wife Barbara Gilchrist, a disposition, 11 August 1625. [ECA.MBI,4/152]

MOATE, JOHN, an Ensign of the Earl of Dunbarton's Regiment which landed at Kinsale in April 1679. [HMC.Ormonde.ii.219]

MONCREIFF, JAMES, a Captain of the Earl of Dunbarton's Regiment which landed at Kinsale in April 1679, later in Middletown. [HMC.Ormonde.ii.219]

MONCREIFF, THOMAS, a merchant in Diamond Street, Londonderry, 1659. [C]

MONYPENNY, ANDREW, Archdeacon of St Saviour's of Connor, 1630. [CSPI]

MONIPENNY, ARTHUR, in the townlands of Monydoroghmore, County Down, 1659. [C]

MONYPENNY, ARTHUR, of P'sons Hall, County Down, 1663. [PRONI.T407]

MONYPENNY, GEORGE, born in County Down, 1642, brown hair, enlisted as a horseman of the King's Guard in Ireland, 1675. [HMC.Ormonde.ii.237]

MONEYPENNY, JOHN, a gentleman, in Ballyskeagh, County Down, 1659. [C]

MONRO, DANIEL, in the townlands of Ballyloch, County Down, 1659. [C]

MONRO, ROBERT, in the townlands of Cumber, County Down, 1659. [C]

MONTGOMERY, ADAM, in County Down, 17 November 1625. [CPRI]

MONTGOMERY, ALEXANDER, in Ballileek, County Monaghan, will refers to his children Thomas, John, Alexander, Robert, Mathew, Hugh, Elizabeth, Sarah, and Dorcas Irvine, sons-in-law Christopher Irvine and John Moutray, nephew Alexander son of brother Robert Montgomery, James Montgomery a child living at Mrs James Grant's, Ann Montgomery a child living with Margaret Dunbar, Margaret Mullins a servant, Alexander Nesbitt's wife, my godson Alexander Nesbitt jr son of said Alexander, John Corry in Castlecoale, County Fermanagh, Casper Wills in Clunagh, County Roscommon, nephew Colonel Alexander Montgomery, Robert Montgomery in Annarea, George Leslie clerk in Clownish, County Monaghan, Alexander Nesbitt a gentleman in Dublin; witnesses John Gill rector of the parish of Kilmore, County Monaghan, Baptist Johnston a gentleman in Tully, County Monaghan, Archibald Moore an apothecary in Monaghan town, Edward Maine a gentleman in Kilmore, James Irvin doctor of physic in Inniskilling, County Fermanagh, Thomas More a servant, William Devall,and James Bowden clerks to Bruen Worthington NP in Dublin, probate 18 April 1722. [DRD]

MONTGOMERY, DAVID, a tenant in Bangor town, County Down, 1681. [HM]

MONTGOMERY, GEORGE, in Ballylessan, Member of the Irish Parliament for the borough of Newton Ards in 1640. [MM]

MONTGOMERIE, Lady ELIZABETH, later Viscountess Ards, died 15 May 1623. [LC.1582]

MONTGOMERIE, Sir HUGH, of Newton, County Down, husband of Lady Elizabeth Montgomerie, an indenture of the Manor House of Gray Abbey, 28 August 1610; Sir Hugh, later Viscount Ards died 15 May 1636. [LC.1582][CPRI]

MONTGOMERY, HUGH, Member of the Irish Parliament for the borough of Newton Ards in 1634. [MM]

MONTGOMERY of the Ards, Lord Viscount HUGH, in Newtown, Barony of the Ards, County Down, 1659. [C]

MONTGOMERY, HUGH, a gentleman in the townlands of Ballymalady, County Down, 1659. [C]

MONTGOMERY, HUGH, parish of Newtown, Barony of The Ards, County Down, 1659. [C]

MONTGOMERY, HUGH, in Knockakeelty, Londonderry, 1659. [C]

MONTGOMERY, HUGH, in Dublin, a letter, 1670. [NRS.GD3.5.717]

MONTGOMERY, HUGH, a tenant in Drumgirvin, County Down, 1681. [HM]

MONTGOMERY, HUGH, a tenant in Ballywaltertown, County Down, 1681. [HM]

MONTGOMERY, HUGH, tenant of Ballylimpt and Ballynagown, County Down, in 1681. [HM]

MONTGOMERY, HUGH, a tenant in Ballymagown, The Ards, County Down, 1681. [HM]

MONTGOMERY, HUGH, Earl of Mount Alexander, will refers to his brother Henry Montgomery and his son Thomas,

his cousin James Montgomery and his son William, cousin
Edmundston Montgomery brother of the said James, cousin Mrs
Jane Shaw and her daughter Sarah Shaw or Montgomery,
cousin Mr Justice Caulfield, friend Charles Campbell, Mrs Jane
Meredith a servant, John Meredith a servant, James Johnston a
mariner in Donaghadee, and John Hepperson a glover;
witnesses Patrick Hamilton, Hugh Clement, Alexander Laing,
William Parry a gentleman in Dublin, and John Gregson,
probate 23 March 1716. [DRD]

MONTGOMERY, HUGH, in Derrygonely, County
Fermanagh, will refers to his wife, their children Nicholas,
Hugh, Richard, Jane, Margaret, Sidney, Sarah and her husband
Brockill Green, brother Robert Montgomery of Derrybrusk,
John Corry of Castle Cole, County Fermanagh; witnesses
Robert Weir in Monaghan, John Trotter in Robinstown, County
Fermanagh, Alexander Atchison in Corryard, County
Fermanagh, Alexander Nesbitt a gentleman in Dublin and his
servant Daniel Byrne, probate8 March 1722. [DRD]

MONTGOMERY, JAMES, of Ruskie in County Fermanagh,
granted Malcolm, Archbishop of Cashel, various lands in
County Fermanagh on 10 May 1626. [CPRI]

MONTGOMERY, JAMES, Bishop of Clogher, 10 April
1629. [CPRI]

MONTGOMERY, JAMES, in the townlands of Cumber,
County Down, 1659. [C]

MONTGOMERY, JOHN, in Mullagh, Londonderry, 1659.
[C]

MONTGOMERY, JOHN, a gentleman in Corshendunyman,
parish of Donoghmore, Barony of Raphoe, County Donegal,
1659. [C]

MONTGOMERY, NICHOLAS, a gentleman in Derrisbrooke, County Fermanagh, 1659. [C]

MONTGOMERY, ROBERT, of Hazelhead in Scotland, granted Robert Montgomery of Rouskie the younger, various lands in County Fermanagh on 6 August 1623. [CPRI]

MONTGOMERY, ROBERT, granted his second son James Montgomery lands in County Fermanagh on 13 August 1623. [CPRI]

MONTGOMERY, ROBERT, master of the Jane of Fairlie, was captured by Parliamentary forces when bound from Nantes, France, to Dublin in 1642. [TNA.HCA13.58.172/235]

MONTGOMERY, THOMAS, of Scotland, now dwelling in Newtown, in the higher Clandeboys, County Down, granted to James Cowper of Nether Mains, residing at Comber, County Down, and his wife Alice, half of the lands of Ballyhosker, in the Great Ards; to hold in fee-farm of Sir Hugh Montgomery, 6 February 1609. [CPRI]

MONTGOMERY, WILLIAM, a gentleman in Movilla, Barony of the Ards, County Down, 1659. [C]

MONTGOMERY, WILLIAM, in Gray Abbey, parish of Gray Abbey, Barony of The Ards, County Down, in 1659. [C]

MONTGOMERY, WILLIAM, in Rosemount, Member of the Irish Parliament for the borough of Newton Ards in 1661. [MM]

MONTGOMERY, WILLIAM, tenant in the water-mill of Dundonell, County Down, in 1681. [HM]

MONTGOMERY, WILLIAM, of Rosemount, County Down,

a bond for £5 sterling with Thomas Inglis a merchant in Edinburgh, 23 August 1683. [NRS.GD1.189.16]

MONTGOMERY, WILLIAM, a merchant in Dublin, was admitted as a burgess and guilds-brother of Glasgow on 4 January 1717. [GBR]

MONTGOMERT, Captain, of Craigbonnie, Donaghadee, 1715. [NRS.AC9.537]

MOORE, ARCHIBALD, of Portaferry, County Down, 1663. [PRONI.T307]

MOORE, ARCHIBALD, a tenant in Ballywaltertown, County Down, 1681. [HM]

MOOR, CHICHESTER, in Antrim, heir to his grand-father James Moor of Kilchivan who died in January 1731, in 1732. [NRS.S/H]

MOORE, HUGH, a tenant in Bangor town, County Down, 1681. [HM]

MOORE, JAMES, tenant of Roddins and Dunover, County Down, in 1681. [HM]

MOORE, JAMES, tenant in Tullyhalbert, County Down, 1681. [HM]

MOORE, JAMES, tenant in Carrickmanan, County Down, 1681. [HM]

MOORE, JOHN, tenant in the Church Quarter of Dundonell, County Down, in 1681. [HM]

MOORE, JOHN, a tenant in Hollywood Town, County Down, in 1681. [HM]

MOORE, ROBERT, of Whitechurch, was granted patent of denization on 5 July 1631. [CPRI]

MOORE, ROBERT, a tenant in Canlige near Bangor, County Down, in 1681. [HM]

MOORE, WILLIAM, of Ballybregagh, and Jane his wife, were granted patent of denization on 5 July 1631. [CPRI]

MOOR, WILLIAM, from Antrim, an indentured servant bound from Liverpool to America in January 1698. [LRO]

MOORE, ..., a widow, a tenant in Ballywaltertown, County Down, 1681. [HM]

MORRISON, RICHARD, master of the <u>Northsbore of Londonderry</u> bound for Portugal, arrested and imprisoned in Southampton, England, charged with trading with France in 1705. [TNA.SP42.120.61; SP44.105.120]

MOUTRAY, JOHN, a gentleman in Glen Colmkill, parish of Killcar, Barony of Boylagh and Banagh, County Donegal, 1659. [C]

MUIR, HEW, in Ridweill, within the Kingdom of Scotland, lastly in the Kingdom of Ireland, testament, 8 July 1645, Glasgow. [NRS]

MUIRHEAD, GEORGE, a soldier of Colonel Bayley's Regiment, 22 February 1648. [HMC.Ormonde.ii.70]

MUNROE, ALEXANDER, Lieutenant Colonel of the Earl of Dunbarton's Regiment which landed at Kinsale in April 1679. [HMC.Ormonde.ii.219]

MUNROE, ANDREW, a Grenadier Captain of the Earl of

Dunbarton's Regiment which landed at Kinsale in April 1679, later in Bandon. [HMC.Ormonde.ii.219]

MUNRO, Mrs MARGARET, in Carrickfergus, a letter, 12 October 1713. [TCD.750.1471]

MURCHIE, ARCHIBALD, master of the Isobel of Belfast in Wemyss, Fife, bound for Belfast, 26 March 1667. [NRS.E72.9.3]

MURDAGH, ANDREW, born in Killileagh, County Down, a blacksmith, took the Oath of Allegiance and Supremacy to King Charles II, on 23 September 1670.

MURDOCH, JAMES, a soldier of Colonel Bayley's Regiment, 22 February 1648. [HMC.Ormonde.ii.70]

MURDOCH, PATRICK, master of the Greyhound of Londonderry, 1614. [UPB.12]

MURDOCH, ROBERT, a soldier of Colonel Bayley's Regiment, 22 February 1648. [HMC.Ormonde.ii.70]

MURDOCH, ROBERT, late of Connor in County Antrim, testament, 1708, Comm. Edinburgh. [NRS]

MURDOCH, ROBERT, born 1657, a merchant in Larne, died 5 January 1742. [Larne gravestone, County Antrim]

MURRAY, Colonel ADAM, commander of a regiment at the defence of Londonderry, where he personally killed the French General de Maumont who had been sent to support the forces of King James, later a Lieutenant Colonel in Lord Charlemont's regiment, died in February 1705, his widow Marie Murray petitioned Queen Anne on behalf of herself and her four children. [TNA.SP44.242.7-8]

MURRAY, ARCHIBALD, an Ensign of the Earl of Dunbarton's Regiment which landed at Kinsale in April 1679. [HMC.Ormonde.ii.219]

MURRAY, CHARLES, a gentleman in Drumbeg townland, parish of Inver, Barony of Boylagh and Banagh, County Donegal, 1659. [C]

MURRAY, CHARLES, Adjutant of the Earl of Dunbarton's Regiment which landed at Kinsale in April 1679. [HMC.Ormonde.ii.219]

MURRAY, CHARLES, in Muckross, Barony of Boylagh and Bannagh, County Donegal, refers to wife Frances, executors Alexander Murray of Broughton, Thomas Knox in Mountcharles, Captain Thomas Knox in Lougheask, and his brother-in-law Captain Albert Nesbitt; witnesses Thomas Knox, John Donnell, Robert Steen, Alexander Nesbitt, and John Taylor, probate 9 March 1713. [DRD]

MURRAY, JAMES, a Captain of the Earl of Dunbarton's Regiment which landed at Kinsale in April 1679, later in Rosse. [HMC.Ormonde.ii.219]

MURRAY, RICHARD, sheriff of County Londonderry before 1672; Captain of a militia troop of horse in County Donegal, 1678. [NRS.GD3.2.29.8; GD10.496]

MURRAY, Sir ROBERT, of Glenmuir, in Castle Murray, parish of Killagtie, Barony of Boylagh and Banagh, County Donegal, 1659. [C]

MURRAY, WILLIAM, in County Meath, 27 May 1628. [CPRI]

MURROW, GEORGE, a Lieutenant of the Earl of

Dunbarton's Regiment which landed at Kinsale in April 1679. [HMC.Ormonde.ii.219]

MURROW, WALTER, a Lieutenant of the Earl of Dunbarton's Regiment which landed at Kinsale in April 1679. [HMC.Ormonde.ii.219]

NAIRNE, D., a secretary in Dublin, a letter, 1689. [NRS.GD406.1.3507]

NAIRN, WILLIAM, a cleric, was appointed vicar of Barnanely alias Killenog, Prebend of Latten, County Tipperary, 12 January 1633. [CPRI]

NAESMITH, JOHN, born 1701, died 23 April 1789. [Larne gravestone, County Antrim]

NAPIER, ARCHIBALD, a gentleman in Cnockro, Barony of Tireill, County Sligo, 1659. [C]

NAPIER, JOHN, in the parish of Down, Barony of Lecale, County Down, 1659. [C]

NEILL, ADAM, in Droghdult, Ballymoney, 1720. [UJA.VII.10]

NEIL, HENRY, a merchant in Pomp Street, Londonderry, 1659. [C]

NEILSON, ELIZABETH, from Donaghadee, County Down, widow of John Fleming of Coutston a merchant in Glasgow, parents of Christian Fleming and Anna Fleming or Pinkston, testament subscribed 25 February 1719, witnesses Francis McMinn, William Agnew, and Florence McCarthy, Commissariat of Glasgow. [NRS][Hamilton Papers mss] [FIB.II.386]

NELSON, ..., a widow, a tenant in Bangor town, County Down, in 1681. [HM]

NESBIT, ANDREW, in the parish of Inver, Barony of Boylagh and Banagh, County Donegal, 1659. [C]

NESBITT, ALBERT, in Toberdally, King's County, his will refers to his late wife Thomasina, their children James, Gifford, Duke, Frances, Lettice, Hellen, Abigail, Thomasina, and Margaret, his sisters Ann, Margaret, Elizabeth, Jane and Catherine, his brothers George, William and Alexander, his cousin Thomas Nesbitt, Simon the Bishop of Elphin, Lord Rochfort, William Conolly, John Wakely, John Moore, Reverend Joseph Graves, Mrs Lettice Loftus, Edward Bermingham, Colley Lyons, his brother in law John Nesbitt, James Collins, James Mills a tenant, John Eaton; witnesses Andrew Calderwood a gentleman in Dublin, and his wife Anna, Alice Nesbitt a widow in Dublin, James Collins a gentleman in King's County, and Henry Buckley, probate 29 March 1720. [DRD]

NESBITT, Reverend GEORGE, Rector of Inniskeel, 1695, a letter, 9 December 1702. [TCD.750/964]

NESBIT, JAMES, in the parish of Inver, Barony of Boylagh and Banagh, County Donegal, 1659. [C]

NESBIT, JOHN, a gentleman in Rathkeylan, County Fermanagh, 1659. [C]

NESMITH, JAMES, in Pomp Street, Londonderry, 1659. [C]

NEVIN, THOMAS, a gentleman in Drumchay, parish of Newton, Barony of the Ards, County Down, 1659. [C]

NEVIN, THOMAS, a gentleman in Ballycoplan, parish of Donaghadee, Barony of the Ards, County Down, 1659. [C]

NICHOLSON, GILBERT, in Dublin, will, 1709. [DRD]

NICHOLSON, HUGH, a tenant in Bangor town, County Down, in 1681. [HM]

NICHOLSON, JOHN, a gentleman in Castleconnor, Barony of Tireagh, County Sligo, 1659. [C]

NICHOLSON, ROBERT, master of the Marigold of Ballintogher, 1614. [UPB.108]

NIMMO, WILLIAM, in Raphoe, letters, 1701. [TCD.750.800/804/808/839.]

NISBET, ALEXANDER, in Dublin, was granted a Crown Charter of Skirling on 26 July 1727. [NRS.RGS.17.115][ECA.MBVI.bundle 158/6029]

NISBIT, ANDREW, a gentleman in Killingrodan, parish of Killamarde, Barony of Boylagh and Banagh, County Donegal, 1659. [C]

NISBIT, ANDREW, a gentleman in Largimore, parish of Killcarr, Barony of Boylagh and Banagh, County Donegal, 1659. [C]

NISBITT, HUGH, in Tullydonell, letters, 1701-1702. [TCD.750.811/825/941]

NISBIT, Captain JOHN, in Tillidonnell, parish of Raphoe, County Donegal, 1659. [C]

O'CONNACHER, CORMACK, an Irish gentleman at the Court of Mary, Queen of Scots, in April 1566. [ATS.XII.49]

OGILVIE, Reverend WILLIAM, died 1712, husband of Jane Agnew. [Larne gravestone, County Antrim]

ORR, ISABEL, died in 1696, widow of Hugh Nicolson of Ballenaghie. [Old Abbey Church gravestone, Bangor, County Down]

ORR, JOHN, deceased in Ireland, son of the umquhile Thomas Orr in Barcosh, testament, 1629, Comm. Glasgow. [NRS]

ORR, PATRICK, a tenant in Ballywaltertown, County Down, 1681. [HM]

ORR, PATRICK, in Tullynewy, in the Barony of Kilconway, 1720. [UJA.VII.11]

ORR, THOMAS, a tenant in Bangor, County Down, 1681. [HM]

ORR, WALTER, master of the Janet of Mongavlin, trading between Londonderry and Scotland, 1615. [UPB.30]

OSBURNE, ALEXANDER, a minister of the Gospel in Dublin, late in Montgomery's toun, Ayrshire, testament 13 February 1690. Commissariat of Glasgow. [NRS]

PARKER, ALEXANDER, a tenant in Bangor town, County Down, in 1681. [HM]

PARKS, JOHN, born 1608, a merchant from Carrickfergus, County Antrim, a witness, April 1639. [TNA.HCA.

PATERSON, ADAM, servant to William Montgomerie a merchant in Dublin, was admitted as a burgess and guilds-brother of Glasgow on 24 July 1717. [GBR]

PATERSON, JANET, relict of James Holme, in Ireland, see Crown Charter, 1644. [RGS.IX.1500]

PATERSON, JOHN, a gentleman in Drumrisk, parish of Devonish, County Fermanagh, 1659. [C]

PATTERSON, JOHN, a tenant in Ballywaltertown, County Down, 1681. [HM]

PATERSON, JOHN, a tenant in Bangor town, County Down, 1681. [HM]

PATON, HENRY, a gentleman in Bellibo, parish of Clandevadock, Barony of Killmccrenan, County Donegal, 1659. [C]

PEACOCK, JOHN, in County Down, 1610. [LC.1582]

PEARSON, ARCHIBALD, a gentleman in Castle Murray, parish of Killagtie, Barony of Boylagh and Banagh, County Donegal, 1659. [C]

PEARSON, DAVID, in County Donegal, 19 May 1693. [NRS.GD1.510.112]

PEEBLES, CATHERINE, wife of Thomas Boyd, died 1 November 1615. [Derryveighan gravestone, County Antrim]

PEEBLES, JOHN, the younger of Pethirland, residing in the parish of Balliemony, County Antrim, married Janet Campbell, eldest daughter of Reverend Alexander Campbell minister at Stevenston, Ayrshire, in Ireland. However, the marriage was dissolved by Andrew Monypennie commissary to Robert Bishop of Down because Janet was married to James Bryding now deceased. The divorce was read and published in the parish kirk of Ballimonie by Thomas Taylor a Notary Public. Reference to John Peebles the elder, in Pethirland, in the parish of Beith, bailliary of Cunningham. The registration of renunciation was registered in Irvine, Ayrshire, 13 November 1632. [Ayrshire Register of Sasines, volume V]

PETICRUE, JAMES, a tenant in Hollywood Town, County Down, in 1681. [HM]

PETTIGREW, JOHN, a tenant in Bangor town, County Down, 1681. [HM]

PIERSON, ALEXANDER, a Lieutenant of the Earl of Dunbarton's Regiment which landed at Kinsale in April 1679. [HMC.Ormonde.ii.219]

POLLOCK, DAVID, in Killeleagh townlands, County Down, 1659. [C]

POLLOCK, JOHN, in Dublin, a deed, 1714. [NRS.RD3.142.42]

POTTINGER, E., master of the Insequin of Belfast in 1661. [BMF.130]

POTTINGER, THOMAS, tenant of Ballymacart, Hollywood, County Down, in 1681. [HM]

PRESSLY, SIMON, a gentleman in Ballyvoyla, parish of Drumully, County Fermanagh, 1659. [C]

PRESTON, DAVID, quartermaster of the Earl of Dunbarton's Regiment which landed at Kinsale in April 1679. [HMC.Ormonde.ii.219]

PRESTON, JOHN, a Captain of the Earl of Dunbarton's Regiment which landed at Kinsale in April 1679. [HMC.Ormonde.ii.219]

PRICE, RANDOLPH, a tenant in Bangor town, County Down, 1681. [HM]

PURDY, ..., a widow, a tenant in Bangor town, County Down, 1681. [HM]

RAMSAY, JOHN, master of the James of Donaghadee trading with Loch Fyne in Scotland during 1665. [PRONI.MIC19.1]

RANDALL, JAMES, in Droghdult, Ballymoney, 1720. [UJA.VII.10]

RANNALEES, PAUL, of Killieleaghie, County Down, owner of a cellar in the High Street of Edinburgh, a disposition, 19 July 1642. [ECA.MB.II.bundle 24/977]

RAYNOLDS, PAUL, of Bangor, was granted patent of denization on 5 July 1631. [CPRI]

REA, HUGH, a tenant in Bangor town, County Down, 1681. [HM]

READ, ALEXANDER, a tenant in Hollywood Town, County Down, in 1681. [HM]

READ, JAMES, a merchant in Newry, County Down, his will refers to his son James and his wife Isabel Heron, his daughter Jane, his daughter Mary and her husband Thomas Assop and their children, his young daughter Sarah, his sister Margaret, his son William, Nicholas Bagnell, Robert Murdoch and John McMahon tenants; witnesses Robert Murdoch a merchant in Newry, Robert Gordon a merchant in Newry, James McCullan a schoolmaster in Dublin, and John Camak, probate 25 February 1720, [DRD]

READ, JOHN, tenant of Ballyhalbert Mill, County Down, in 1681. [HM]

REID, DAVID, tenant of Portavogy and Green Isle, County Down, 1681. [HM]

REID, DAVID, tenant of Glasscragh and St John's Quarter in County Down, in 1681. [HM]

REED, HUGH, in Corstoun Kill, Liberty of Coleraine, 1720. [UJA.VII.10]

REID, JOHN, dwelling in the kingdom of Ireland, sold lands to Thomas Fergusson a smith in Herne, charter dated at Ayr, Scotland, on 24 January 1626. [NRS.CH1.186.8]

REID, THOMAS, in Auchendowie, County Londonderry, 23 November 1665. [NRS.GD1.693.13]

REED, THOMAS, in Corstoun Kill, Liberty of Coleraine, 1720. [UJA.VII.10]

REID, Mr WILLIAM, minister at Belliwalter, was granted a Crown Charter of the lands of Daldilling on 22 July 1681. [NRS.RGS.10.217]

RITCHART, PATRICK, in Ireland, 1611, a debtor mentioned in the testament of Charles Campbell in Vicarton, Girvan, Ayrshire, confirmed, Comm. Glasgow. 1612. [NRS]

RITCHIE, ALEXANDER, a tenant in Bangor town, County Down, in 1681. [HM]

RITCHIE, ..., a widow, a tenant in Bangor town, County Down, in 1681. [HM]

ROBB, JOHN, a tenant in Hollywood Town, County Down, in 1681. [HM]

ROBINSON, DAVID, born 1683, died 22 May 1765. [Raloo gravestone, County Antrim]

ROBINSON, JOHN, in Killeleagh townlands, County Down, 1659. [C]

ROBINSON, JOHN, in Hollywood, County Down, in 1681. [HM]

ROLLO, ARCHIBALD, a Captain of the Earl of Dunbarton's Regiment which landed at Kinsale in April 1679, later in Clonakilty. [HMC.Ormonde.ii.219]

RONALD, PAUL, of Killileaghe, County Down, a deed, 24 April 1637; disposition of a cellar on the High Street of Edinburgh, 19 July 1642. [ECA.MBI.18/725; 24/977]

ROSS, GEORGE, of Karney, born 1649, died 27 December 1704, husband of Ursula Ross or Hamilton, born 1647, died 26 February 1730. [Slanes parish gravestone, The Ards, County Down]

ROSS, GEORGE, a gentleman in Ballow parish of Bangor, Barony of the Ards, County Down, 1659. [C]

ROSS, GEORGE, a tenant in Grange of Witter, The Ards, County Down, 1681. [HM]

ROSS, HUGH, a gentleman in Derrycannon, parish of Kilnawly, County Fermanagh, 1659. [C]

ROSS, JAMES, petitioned King Charles I for a grant of 2000 acres in Ireland, 1634. [CSPI]

ROSS, JAMES, a gentleman in Portavo, Ballyfutherly and the Coplan Isles parish of Bangor, Barony of the Ards, County Down, 1659. [C]

ROSS, JAMES, a tenant in Portavo and Ballow, near Bangor, County Down, in 1681. [HM]

ROSS, JAMES, tenant of Ballyknockgavey, Ballykeele, and Ballyregan, Hollywood, County Down, in 1681. [HM]

ROSS, JAMES, born 1705, died 21 April 1738. [Blaris gravestone, County Down]

ROSS, JOHN, a gentleman in the townlands of Lishbraden, County Down, 1659. [C]

ROSS, JOHN, a merchant in Coleraine, husband of Dorothea .... born 1671, died 11 December 1713. [Ballywillin gravestone, County Antrim]

ROSS, ROBERT, a gentleman in Anninare, County Femanagh, in 1659. [C]

ROSS, ROBERT, a gentleman in Portavo, Ballyfutherly and the Coplan Isles parish of Bangor, Barony of the Ards, County Down, 1659. [C]

ROSSE, ROBERT, of Ballihenry, County Down, 1663. [PRONI.T307]

ROSS, ROBERT, a tenant in Cullintragh Mill, County Down, 1681. [HM]

ROSS, WILLIAM, a gentleman in Anninare, County Fermanagh, in 1659. [C]

ROSS, WILLIAM, a gentleman in Derrycannon, parish of Kilnawly, County Fermanagh, 1659. [C]

ROWAN, ANDREW, in Clough, in the Barony of Kilconway, 1720. [UJA.VII.11]

RUSSELL, GAWEN, a tenant in Hollywood Town, County Down, in 1681. [HM]

RUSSELL, GEORGE, of Rathmullen, County Down, and George his grandson and heir, 9 December 1628. [CPRI]

RUSSELL, WILLIAM, a tenant in Hollywood Town, County Down, in 1681. [HM]

RUTHERFORD, THOMAS, an Ensign of the Earl of Dunbarton's Regiment which landed at Kinsale in April 1679. [HMC.Ormonde.ii.219]

RUTHVEN, JOHN, a Lieutenant of Dunbarton's Regiment which landed at Kinsale in April 1679. [HMC.Ormonde.ii.219]

RYND, DAVID, a gentleman in Enniskillen, County Fermanagh, 1659. [C]

SANDERSON, ROBERT, of Castle Sanderson in County Down, a decree re the lands of Balvie, versus Sir Humphry Colquhoun of Luss, 1 February 1710. [ECA.MBV.bundle 140/5476]

SAVAGE, HUGH, tenant in Ballyknockan, Hollywood town, County Down, in 1681. [HM]

SCOTT, ANDREW, an Ensign of the Earl of Dunbarton's Regiment which landed at Kinsale in April 1679. [HMC.Ormonde.ii.219]

SCOTT, GEORGE, a gentleman in Drumslavage, Monaghan, in 1659. [C]

SCOTT, Reverend GIDEON, Rector of Tamlaght-Finlagan, County Londonderry, letters, 1694, 1701. [TCD.750.850/869/1359.]

SCOT, HUGH, of Dunethry, born 1648, died 24 June 1740. [Donegore gravestone, County Antrim]

SCOT, Reverend HUGH, born 1705, died 26 March 1736, grandson of the above Hugh Scot. [Donegore gravestone, County Antrim]

SCOTT, JOHN, a Lieutenant of the Earl of Dunbarton's Regiment which landed at Kinsale in April 1679. [HMC.Ormonde.ii.219]

SCOTT, MARGARET, a tenant in Ballywaltertown, County Down, 1681. [HM]

SCOTT, THOMAS, a Lieutenant of the Earl of Dunbarton's Regiment which landed at Kinsale in April 1679. [HMC.Ormonde.ii.219]

SCOTT, WILLIAM, gauger and packer of the ports of Dublin, Skerries, Malahide, and Wicklow, 4 February 1629. [CPRI]

SCOTT, WILLIAM, in Aghanahoula, Monaghan, in 1659. [C]

SCOTT, WILLIAM, tenant of Ballymaglane Itagh, parish of Magredrill, Kinelarty Barony, County Down, 1703. [PRONI.D1854.2.29A]

SCOTT, WILLIAM, a gentleman in Aunahagh, County Monaghan, will refers to his eldest son John Scott, his mother Mary Scott married to Cornet Edward Forster; witnesses Joseph Greer a weaver in Annahagh, John Owen a gentleman in Killmore, Henry Owen a gentleman in Killmore, County Meath, Brien Worthington a Notary Public in Dublin, Francis Forster a gentleman in Quigillagh, County Monaghan, probate 20 January 1721. [DRD]

SCOTT, ..., a widow, a tenant in Ballywaltertown, County Down, 1681. [HM]

SEATON, CHRISTOPHER, a soldier wounded in Ireland 'for religion and the present king' was granted 18 shillings by Inverkeithing Kirk Session on 10 June 1690. [Inverkeithing Kirk Session Records, Fife, Scotland]

SEATON, THOMAS, tenant in County Fermanagh, robbed and killed by rebels in 1641. [PRONI.MIC.8.2]

SEMPILL, LEVENIS, in town of Letterkenny, parish of Cornwall, Barony of Killmccrenan, County Donegal, 1659. [C]

SEMPLE, JOHN, a mariner from Carrickfergus, died aboard the <u>America</u> in Jamaica, probate 1694. [PCC]

SEMPLE, WILLIAM, a non-conformist minister in Ireland, petitioned King Charles II in 1669. [CSPI]

SETON, Sir JOHN, was granted the Manor of Monelagan or Balleleghan, in County Longford, on 8 August 1628. [CPRI]

SHAW, FRANCIS, in Strabane, 1613, brother of Robert Shaw of Bargarrane. [NRS.GD86.405]

SHAW, HUGH, in Newtown, Barony of the Ards, County Down, 1659. [C]

SHAW, JOHN, in Ballywitticock, parish of Newtown, Barony of the Ards, County Down, 1659. [C]

SHAW, JOHN, a tenant in Bangor town, County Down, 1681. [HM]

SHAW, JOHN, a gentleman in Ballytweedy, County Antrim, his will refers to his children Helen and Henry, his brother Thomas Shaw of Ballyminsttragh, his kinsman James Crawford of Ballysavage, William McCulloch of Piedmont, all in County Antrim; witnesses William Agnew a gentleman in Kilwaughter,

William Cunningham a surgeon in Ballyrobin, John McNeily farmer in Carngrany, Josh Wilson a gentleman in Antrim, all in County Antrim, and Daniel Kelly clerk to Robert Donaldson a gentleman in Dublin, probate 22 April 1729. [DRD]

SHAW, MARGARET, in Greenock, Renfrewshire, relict of William Shaw, Provost of Newton in Ireland, testament, 4 August 1666, Comm. Glasgow. [NRS]

SHAW, PATRICK, brother-german of Lady Elizabeth Montgomerie, 1610. [LC.1582]

SHAW, PATRICK, a gentleman in the parish of Killaid, Barony of Massereen, County Antrim, will refers to his daughter Mary, a minor, and her guardians – his father William Shaw of Bush, Patrick Agnew of Killwaughter, and his brother John Shaw of Bush, his father-in-law William Shaw of Ganaway, his brother John Shaw of Bush, brother Thomas Shaw, and his kinsman William McCulloch of Grogan; witnesses Francis Iredell a gentleman in Dublin, Victor Ferguson a doctor of physics in Belfast, John Crafford a yeoman in Bush, County Antrim, and Robert Donaldson, probate 29 August 1715. [DRD]

SHAW, ROBERT, born 1586, from Londonderry, a mariner aboard the Mary of Coleraine, a witness before the High Court of the Admiralty of England in April 1637. [TNA.HCA.53.126]

SHAW, ROBERT, a merchant traveller betwixt Scotland and Ireland, a deed, 1715. [NRS.RD2.104.489]

SHAW, WILLIAM, in parish of Newtown, Barony of the Ards, County Down, 1659. [C]

SHAW, WILLIAM, a tenant in Calnord, County Down, 1681. [HM]

SHAW, WILLIAM, of Ballyganway, County Down, a lease, 1681. [PRONI.D24]

SHAW, WILLIAM, a tenant in Carrowdorne and Ballymontesney, County Down, 1681. [HM]

SHAW, WILLIAM, in Ballygonway, County Down, will refers to his wife, his son John Shaw, his daughter Rose Haven, his daughter Frances wife of Patrick Shaw, his daughter Anne wife of Cornelius Crimble, grandson Ganaway son of Cornelius Crimble, grand-daughter Jane Crimble, sister Elizabeth Gillespie, nephew Hugh Gillespie, William Shaw in Bush, County Antrim, and the children of William Catherwood of Newtown; witnesses John O'Neill in Dunmore, County Antrim, William Catherwood a gentleman in Newtown, County Down, William Colvill a gentleman in Dublin, and William Dempster, probate 25 August 1710. [DRD]

SHAW, WILLIAM, of Gannay, Ireland, a deed, 1715. [NRS.RD4.117.808]

SHEARER, ..., a widow, a tenant in Ballywaltertown, County Down, 1681. [HM]

SIM, JAMES, a tenant in Hollywood Town, County Down, in 1681. [HM]

SIME, JAMES, a gentleman in Magherireagh, parish of Donoghmore, Barony of Raphoe, County Donegal, 1659. [C]

SIME, JOHN, a gentleman in Magherireagh, parish of Donoghmore, Barony of Raphoe, County Donegal, 1659. [C]

SIMPSON, JANET, wife of Alexander Simpson in Hillsborough, Ireland, only daughter and heir of William Simpson a gardener in Erskine, Renfrewshire, a sasine re land

in Haddington, East Lothian, 3 March 1705.
[ECA.MBVI.bundle 176/6941]

SIMPSON, ROBERT, a tenant in Ballywaltertown, County Down, 1681. [HM]

SIMPSON, WILLIAM, a tenant in Bangor town, County Down, 1681. [HM]

SINCLAIR, JOHN, in Omagh, County Tyrone, letters, 1700-1702. [TCD.750.699/900]

SINCLAIR, Sir WILLIAM, in King's County, 3 August 1627. [CPRI]

SLOAN, ALEXANDER, in the townlands of Lissnagh, County Down, 1659. [C]

SLOANE, JAMES, of the Inner Temple of London, formerly of Rowvagh, County Down, a deed of factory, 1679. [NRS.GD109.1898]

SLOAN, JAMES, a tenant of Ballygarven, Ballyfister, and Bowreagh, County Down, 1681. [HM]

SLOAN, JAMES, tenant of Ballymazer, Hollywood, County Down, in 1681. [HM]

SLOANE, JOHN, master of the Greyhound of Londonderry, 1615. [UPB.20]

SLOIS, JOHN, master of the Greyhound of Londonderry, trading between Londonderry and Rouen, France, 1614. [UPB.12]

SMITH, DAVID, a Presbyterian and a merchant burgess of Belfast from 1690 until 1705. [BMF]

104

SMITH, JAMES, a brewer in Belfast, will refers to his wife Hanna, their children James, Sarah, Elizabeth, and Mary, his brother Nathan Smith, William Stevenson of Ballymacart, County Down, Daniel Mussenden a merchant in Belfast, James Park a merchant in Belfast, John Gregg of Glenavey, County Antrim; witnesses Mathew Davison, John Wilson, Edward Logan all yeomen in Belfast, probate 10 November 1729. [DRD]

SMITH, JOHN, a tenant in Bangor town, County Down, 1681. [HM]

SMITH, ROBERT, a tenant in Bangor town, County Down, 1681. [HM]

SMITH, ..., a merchant in Belfast, was admitted as a burgess of Edinburgh on 25 August 1704. [REB]

SOMERVILL, JAMES, in Dublin, letters, 1701. [TCD.750.779/793/798/803/813.]

SOMERVILLE, THOMAS, a gentleman in Drumnadown, parish of Devonish, County Fermanagh, 1659. [C]

SOMERVILLE, WILLIAM, a barber in Dublin, was admitted as a burgess and guilds-brother of Glasgow in 1717. [GBR]

SPENCE, JAMES, minister at Castlemartine in Ireland, son of Alexander Spence a minister at Birnie, a deed, 1715. [NRS.RD3.146.574]

SPOTSWOOD, Sir HENRY, in the Barony of Clogher, County Tyrone, 2 July 1629. [CPRI]

SPOTSWOOD, Sir JOHN, was made a free denizen of Ireland and granted land in County Leitrim, 25 May 1625. [CPRI]

SPREULL, ARCHIBALD, a gentleman in Boggach and Stranorlaghan, parish of Raphoe, Barony of Raphoe, County Donegal, 1659. [C]

SPREULL, JOHN, a gentleman in Boggach and Stranorlaghan, parish of Raphoe, Barony of Raphoe, County Donegal, 1659. [C]

STEVENSON, JAMES, a soldier of Colonel Bayley's Regiment, 22 February 1648. [HMC.Ormonde.ii.70]

STEVENSON, JOHN, a tenant in Part Killare near Bangor, County Down, in 1681. [HM]

STEWART, ALEXANDER, a gentleman in the townlands of Killinikin, County Down, 1659. [C]

STEWART, ALEXANDER, in Ballimore, parish of Clandehurka, Barony of Killmccrenan, County Donegal, 1659. [C]

STEWART, ALEXANDER, born 1645, died 20 October 1723, also his wife Elizabeth Fraser, born 1652, died 12 May 1734, parents of Walter Stewart, who died 6 March 1762. [Ballintoy gravestone]

STEWART, ANDREW, a gentleman in Moriss, parish of Templemore, Barony of Killmccrenan, County Donegal, 1659. [C]

STEWART, ANDREW, in Drumnagola, Barony of Carey. 1720. [UJA.VII.11]

STEWART, ANDREW, of Stewarthall, County Tyrone, a deed, 1702. [NRS.RD3.100.219]

STEWART, ARCHIBALD, in Dublin, a letter, 1637. [NRS.GD406.1.359]

STEWART, ARCHIBALD, a gentleman in Ballinacaragh, parish of Templemore, Barony of Killmccrenan, County Donegal, 1659. [C]

STEWART, ARCHIBALD, in Ballentoy, a letter, 21 January 1723. [TCD.750.2025]

STEWART, DANIEL, in Ballynalea, Barony of Carey. 1720. [UJA.VII.11]

STEWART, DAVID, a gentleman, in the parish of Mevagh, Barony of Kilmccrenan, County Donegal, 1659. [C]

STEWART, ELIZABETH, sister and heir of Robert Stewart of Gass, and spouse of Thomas Agnew in Gray Abbey, Ireland, 2 February 1627; 9 March 1627. [NRS.GD25.SEC.8.183; SEC.4.B15/34]

STEWART, GEILLS, relict of Colin Campbell of Ballechirrin, Ireland, a deed, 1702. [NRS.RD2.86.2.17]

STEWART, GEORGE, probably in County Donegal, was granted letters of denization, 19 July 1631. [CPRI]

STEWART, GEORGE, a Lieutenant of the Earl of Dunbarton's Regiment which landed at Kinsale in April 1679. [HMC.Ormonde.ii.219]

STEWART, HENRY, was granted letters patent of denization, and 1560 acres in the precinct of Mountjoy, Barony of Dungannon, County Tyrone, to be called the Manor of Carragan, 3 March 1629. [CPRI]

STEWART, JAMES, of Kilcanny, County Tyrone, 2 July 1629. [CPRI]

STEWART, JAMES, in Mondowy, parish of Ray, Barony of Raphoe, County Donegal, 1659. [C]

STEWART, JAMES, a Lieutenant of the Earl of Dunbarton's Regiment which landed at Kinsale in April 1679. [HMC.Ormonde.ii.219]

STEWART, JAMES, a merchant in Belfast, a deed, 1702. [NRS.RD3.99.2.34]

STEWART, Captain JAMES, in Corkey, Barony of Dunluce, 1720. [UJA.VII.9]

STEWART, JOHN, a resident of the Precinct of Portlogh in 1611, [Carew.Mss.58]; was denizised and granted 1000 acres in the precinct of Portlogh, Barony of Raphoe, County Donegal, to be called the Manor of Stewartscourt, 9 May 1629. [CPRI]

STEWART, JOHN, a gentleman in the townlands of Marran, County Down, 1659. [C]

STEWART, JOHN, in Cowlglee, parish of Ray, Barony of Raphoe, County Donegal, 1659. [C]

STEWART, JOHN, and his son FRANCIS STEWART, in Drumoghell, parish of Ray, Barony of Raphoe, County Donegal, 1659. [C]

STEWART, JOHN FRANCIS, a tenant in McBride's Quarter, Manor of Ballydeine, County Down, 1681. [HM]

STEWART, JOHN, in Leotrim, Barony of Dunluce, 1720. [UJA.VII.10]

STEWART, MATTHEW, probably in County Donegal, was granted letters of denization, 19 July 1631. [CPRI]

STEWART, MATTHEW, a gentleman, in Drumbarn, parish of Ray, Barony of Raphoe, County Donegal, 1659. [C]

STEWART, PATRICK, was granted land in the Barony of Dromahere, County Leitrim, on 14 July 1628. [CPRI]

STEWART, ROBERT, of Haulton, resident in the Precinct of Mountjoy in 1611. [Carew.Mss.58]

STEWART, ROBERT, of Robston, resident in the Precinct of Mountjoy in 1611. [Carew.Mss.58]

STEWART, ROBERT, in Cowlglee, parish of Ray, Barony of Raphoe, County Donegal, 1659. [C]

STEWART, Captain THOMAS, in Magheryhy, parish of Drumhome, Barony of Tirhugh, County Donegal, 1659. [C]

STEWART, THOMAS, in Hamilton, parish of Auchnish, Barony of Killmccrenan, County Donegal, 1659. [C]

STEWART, WALTER, in Anaghculan, County Fermanagh, in 1659. [C]

STEWART, WILLIAM, was granted letters of denization and 1000 acres in Cooleaghy, precinct of Portlogh, Barony of Raphoe, County Donegal, on 7 May 1629. [CPRI]

STEWART, Captain WILLIAM, son of Lord Garlies, was killed at Kilcullin Bridge in 1641. [Drumbeg gravestone, County Down]

STEWART, Sir WILLIAM, letters from Sir Phelim O'Neale, 1641. [CSPI]

STEWART, WILLIAM, in Bellilane, parish of Ray, Barony of Raphoe, County Donegal, 1659. [C]

STEWART, WILLIAM, a tenant in Ballywaltertown, County Down, 1681. [HM]

STEWART, WILLIAM, in Kervecraine, Barony of Dunluce, 1720. [UJA.VII.10]

STEWARD, HARRY, of Barkesmyne, purchased the island of Rathlin in 1585. [Carew mss.1617.188]

STEWARD, JOHN, master of the Post of Londonderry, 1614, and of the Elizabeth of Londonderry, 1615. [UPB.4/20]

STEWARD, WILLIAM, petitioned King Charles I to be granted the Castle of Culmore near Londonderry, 1635. [CSPI]

STIRLING, JAMES, of Knockkerogh, born 1634, died 24 January 1708, husband of Janet Wilson, who died 18 November 1699. [Ballyrashane gravestone, County Antrim]

STIRLING, JOHN, a Lieutenant of the Earl of Dunbarton's Regiment which landed at Kinsale in April 1679. [HMC.Ormonde.ii.219]

STIRLING, ROBERT, in Bangor town, County Down, 1681. [HM]

STIRLING, Reverend ROBERT, died June 1698. [Derrykeighan gravestone, County Antrim]

STORIE, JOHN, corporal of Colonel Bayley's Regiment, 22 February 1648. [HMC.Ormonde.ii.69]

STRACHAN, ALEXANDER, a soldier of Colonel Bayley's Regiment, 22 February 1648. [HMC.Ormonde.ii.70]

STRANG, Mr WILLIAM, minister at Athalie in Ireland, husband of Christian Strang, a disposition of land in Edinburgh to John Sloan a merchant burgess, 16 August 1637; another in favour of John Mitchell a baker burgess of Edinburgh, 16 August 1637. [ECA.MBI.18/738; 19/773]

STRAUGHAN, JAMES, in Radufinore, County Wicklow, will refers to his brother William, his natural son Charles Straughan, his illegitimate children Ann, James, Richard, Bridget and William, probate 3 November 1715. [DRD]

SWADLIN, JOHN, a tenant in Ballymaconnell near Bangor, County Down, in 1681. [HM]

SYERS, JOHN, a tenant in Lisbane, Manor of Ballydeine, County Down, 1681. [HM]

SYMINGTON, JOHN, was granted letters patent of denization and 1000 acres in the precinct of Mountjoy, Barony of Dungannon, County Tyrone, to be called the Manor of Symington, 16 December 1630. [CPRI]

TATE, NINIAN, tenant in the Church Quarter of Dundonell, County Down, in 1681. [HM]

TAYLOR, JOHN, a merchant in Belfast, will refers to his wife, his sons John and Arthur; witnesses George Johnston a merchant in Belfast, Thomas Martin a merchant in Belfast, Robert Henderson a glover in Belfast, and Robert Legg an attorney in Dublin, probate 21 January 1729. [DRD]

THOMSON, ARCHIBALD, with Anthony and John his sons, in Galdinagh, parish of Ray, Barony of Raphoe, County Donegal, 1659. [C]

THOMSON, HEW, a burgess of Londonderry, a creditor of

Jean Campbell, spouse of William Dunlop of Craig in Kilmaurs, Ayrshire, testament, 1621, Comm. Glasgow. [NRS]

THOMSON, HUGH, sometime in Rebegge, County Antrim, now in the Halls of Bargoure,, Ayrshire, a registration of renunciation, 15 November 1642. [Ayrshire Register of Sasines, volume VII]

THOMSON, HUGH, a gentleman in Pump Street, Londonderry, 1659. [C]

THOMSON, JOHN, a merchant in Coleraine, a deed, 1691. [NRS.RD2.74.149]

THOMSON, LEWIS, a merchant in Belfast, a petitioner in 1691. [RPCS.XVI.309]

THOMPSON, ROBERT, a tenant in Bangor town, County Down, in 1681. [HM]

THOMPSON, WILLIAM, a Lieutenant of the Earl of Dunbarton's Regiment which landed at Kinsale in April 1679. [HMC.Ormonde.ii.219]

TODD, RACHEL, in Maddebainey, Liberty of Coleraine, 1720. [UJA.VII.10]

TRAIL, Mrs, a tenant of Granshogh, County Down, 1681. [HM]

TWADELL, JOHN, a shopkeeper in Coleraine, 1659. [C]

TWEED, JOHN, born 1647, died 1719. [Carncastle gravestone, Antrim]

TWEED, ROBERT, born 1670, died 11 December 1759, husband of Margaret Young, born 1672, died 11 January 1740. [Carncastle gravestone, County Antrim]

VANCE, PATRICK, a tenant in Ballywaltertown, County Down, 1681. [HM]

VASSE, HEW, minister at Dunluce, in Ireland, his relict Marion Cunningham testament, 1670, Commissariat of Glasgow. [NRS]

VAS, WILLIAM, a gentleman in the parish of Clandevadock, Barony of Killmccrenan, County Donegal, 1659. [C]

VERNER, BENJAMIN, of Killgavinache, County Antrim, a deed, 1694. [NRS.RD2.77.ii.584]

VERNER, JOHN, a gentleman in the townlands of Drumskea, Drummore, County Down, 1659. [C]

WADDELL, ALEXANDER, a gentleman in the townlands of Banderry, Drummore, County Down, 1659. [C]

WALKER, GEORGE, in Londonderry, a letter, 1689. [NRS.GD406.1.3527]

WALLACE, ALEXANDER, pipe-major of the Earl of Dunbarton's Regiment which landed at Kinsale in April 1679. [HMC.Ormonde.ii.219]

WALLACE, GEORGE, a tenant in Priory House, County Down, 1681. [HM]

WALLACE, HUGH, in Roddins, parish of Ballyharber, Barony of The Ards, County Down, in 1659. [C]

WALLACE, HUGH, tenant of Ballyobtkin, The Ards, County Down, in 1681. [HM]; will refers to his wife Beatrix, their children Alexander, Hans, Beatrix, Jane and Sarah, his brother in law John Hutcheson in Ballyrea, County Armagh; witnesses William Alexander MD in Belfast, Hugh Catherwood surgeon in Kirkistown, County Down, Hugh McWilliam servant to John

Hutcheson in Ballyrea, John Brennand a gentleman in Armagh, and James Reeed, probate 29 November 1716. [DRD]

WALLACE Mr JAMES, a minister in Ulster, to go to Dublin for instructions before moving to Connaught, 12 June 1655. [IC.ii.682]

WALLACE, JAMES, a gentleman in Ballyobikin, parish of Ballywalter, Barony of The Ards, County Down, in 1659. [C]

WALLACE, JAMES, of Brickland, a merchant, born 1700, died 19 May 1763. [Loughbrickland gravestone, Aghaderg]

WALLACE, JOHN, commissioned to undertake the wardship of Randal McDonnell, Viscount Dunluce, 3 March 1630. [CPRI]

WALLACE, NICHOLAS, master of the James of Dublin, from Dublin to Bilbao, Spain, in 1705. [TNA.SP44.390.323]

WALLACE, THOMAS, a gentleman in Tullinadale, parish of Clandevadock, Barony of Killmccrenan, County Donegal, 1659. [C]

WALLACE, WILLIAM, a tenant in Bangor town, County Down, in 1681. [HM]

WALLACE, ..., a widow, a tenant in Hollywood Town, County Down, in 1681. [HM]

WARDEN, ..., a widow, a tenant in Hollywood Town, County Down, in 1681. [HM]

WARDLAW, ARCHIBALD, a gentleman in the townlands of Drumkey, County Down, 1659. [C]

WARDLAW, KATHREN, daughter of James Wardlaw of

Drumkenn, County Down, and spouse of Gilbert Hamilton, a deed, 1714. [NRS.RD2.103.1.623]

WARNOCK, JOHN, a tenant in Ballywaltertown, County Down, 1681. [HM]

WARNOCK, ROBERT, a tenant in Ballywaltertown, County Down, 1681. [HM]

WARNOCK, ..., a widow, in Ballywaltertown, Down, in 1681. [HM]

WATSON, DAVID, Precentor of St Patrick's, Armagh, was presented to the rectory and vicarage of Kilsleve, in the Diocese of Armagh, 7 June 1627, 23 June 1628. [CPRI]

WATSON, EDWARD, merchant in Coleraine, 1615. [UPB.87]

WATSON, JOHN, was appointed Treasurer of the Cathedral of St Patrick's in Armagh on 8 February 1627. [CPRI]

WATSON, JOHN. a tenant in Bangor town, County Down, in 1681. [HM]

WATSON, VALENTINE, a tenant in Bangor town, County Down, 1681. [HM]

WATT, GEORGE, a tenant in Hollywood Town, County Down, in 1681. [HM]

WATT, JOHN, a tenant in Hollywood Town, County Down, in 1681. [HM]

WATT, WILLIAM, a tenant in Hollywood Town, County Down, in 1681. [HM]

WAUCHOPE, JAMES, a gentleman in the townlands of Drummachlist, County Down, 1659. [C]

WAUGH, JAMES, a gentleman in Uttan, parish of Clownish, County Fermanagh, in 1659. [C]

WAUGH, WALTER, in Uttan, parish of Clownish, County Fermanagh, in 1659. [C]

WEIR, ALEXANDER, a gentleman in Ferlagh, parish of Devonish, County Fermanagh, 1659. [C]

WEIR, ROBERT, a gentleman in Magherynagiran, parish of Devonish, County Fermanagh, 1659. [C]

WEIR, ROBERT, a gentleman in Monahan, parish of Devonish, County Fermanagh, 1659. [C]

WEMYSS, Sir JOHN, was murdered before May 1629. [CPRI]

WHITE, ADAM, a non-conformist minister in Ireland, petitioned King Charles II in 1669. [CSPI]

WHYTE, ADAM, minister of the parish of Dunluce, County Antrim, disposed of the lands of Murthorgall in the parish of Lesmahagow, in the Upper Ward of Lanarkshire, to his son George Whyte on 20 May 1699. [NRS.GD1.179.51]

WHITE, HUGH, a tenant in Ballyrea near Bangor, County Down, in 1681. [HM]

WHYTE, JOHN, merchant in Belfast, aboard the Isobel of Belfast in Wemyss, Fife, bound for Belfast, 26 March 1667. [NRS.E72.9.3]

WHITE, JOHN, a Lieutenant of the Earl of Dunbarton's Regiment which landed at Kinsale in April 1679. [HMC.Ormonde.ii.219]

WHITE, SIMON, master of the <u>Kething of Wexford</u> arrived in Glasgow in July 1627. [GBR]

WHITE, WILLIAM, an Ensign of the Earl of Dunbarton's Regiment which landed at Kinsale in April 1679. [HMC.Ormonde.ii.219]

WHITE, ..., the widow, a tenant in Ballywaltertown, County Down, in 1681. [HM]

WHITELAW, KATHERINE, wife of Robert Whitelaw a clerk, was pardoned for the manslaughter of George Amand in County Fermanagh, 7 September 1628. [CPRI]

WHITELAW, ROBERT, Rector of Aghalurcher, was granted lands in the Barony of Clogher, County Tyrone, 29 February 1631. [CPRI]

WHITLAW, JAMES, a tenant in Bangor town, County Down, in 1681. [HM]

WHITLAW, ..., a widow, a tenant in Bangor town, County Down, in 1681. [HM]

WILEY, NATHANIEL, aged 106, died at Clogh near Ballymena on 19 February 1758. 'He was petty constable of Ballymena when King James XII's army marched in 1689 to besiege Londonderry. He used to say, he served two kings in one day; King William in the forenoon, out of love; and King James in the afternoon out of fear'. [SM.20.110]

WILKIN, JOHN, of Carrickfeagh, was granted a fee-farm in Ulster by Sir John Hume of Castle Hume, 1 November 1673. [NRS.GD1.273]

WILLIAMS, GRIETGE, from Ireland, married Hendry

Hendry, a soldier from Orkney, Scotland, in Rotterdam, the Netherlands, on 26 March 1606. [Rotterdam Marriage Register]

WILLIAMSON, DAVID, in Killeleagh townlands, County Down, 1659. [C]

WILLIAMSON, JOHN, born in Conner, County Antrim, a tailor, took the Oath of Allegiance and Supremacy to King Charles II, on 15 December 1668. [Patent Roll 20/29/f7]

WILSON, HUGH, a tenant in Bangor town, County Down, 1681. [HM]

WILSON, Sir JOHN, of Killenure, County Donegal, 20 May 1629. [CPRI]

WILSON, JOHN, in the Barony of Dunluce, 1720. [UJA.VII.10]

WILSON, NATHANIEL, a merchant in Belfast, trading with William Dawson, Provost of Forres, Morayshire, an interdiction by the Customs and Excise, 1720. [Documents of the Province of Moray, Edinburgh, 1895, p.33]

WILSON, ROBERT, was appointed Dean of Ferns on 24 February 1628. [CPRI]

WILSON, WILLIAM, 'a chapman in the county of Cuttoun, Kingdom of Ireland', testament, 19 January 1644, Comm. Glasgow. [NRS]

WISHART, HENRY, servant to Colonel Hamilton, a Captain in Ireland, testament, 16 March 1644, Comm. Glasgow. [NRS]

WISHART, Sir JOHN, with 15 people, in County Fermanagh, 1611. [Carew mss.1611.68]

WISHART, JOHN, in Clontenorin, County Fermanagh, 1659. [C]

WORKMAN, JOHN, born 1696, died 25 April 1717. [Blaris gravestone, County Down]

WORKMAN, ROBERT, born 1692, died 17 January 1737, husband of J. Cary White, died 20 May 1747. [Larne gravestone, County Antrim]

WRAY, WILLIAM, in Fore, County Donegal, will refers to his wife Angel, his son Humphrey husband of Ann Brook, son Henry husband of Joan Jackson, sons-in-law James Sinclair and George Knox, daughter Rebecca Babington, the heirs of Richard Porter, John Richardson, my servants Samuel Densmoore and Thomas Blair, Mrs Ann Sinclair, Captain Henry Hart, William Finlay in Drumnatinny, Hugh Hamill, William Sampson, William Godfrey, Benjamin Galland, John Humble, John Evans, Captain George Hamilton; witnesses George Knox, Patrick Densmoore, Samuel Densmoore, Humphrey Wray and Thomas Knox, 1 December 1710.[DRD],

WRIGHT, SAMUEL, a tenant in Hollywood Town, County Down, in 1681. [HM]

WYLLIE, ALEXANDER, a tenant in Bangor town, County Down, in 1681. [HM]

YEATES, JOHN, born in Leedon, West Lothian, a trunk-maker in Ireland, took the Oath of Allegiance and Supremacy to King Charles II, on 29 July 1672.

YOUNG, FRANCIS, a soldier of Colonel Bayley's Regiment, 22 February 1648. [HMC.Ormonde.ii.69]

YOUNG, GEORGE, a soldier of Colonel Bayley's Regiment, 22 February 1648. [HMC.Ormonde.ii.69]

YOUNG, HENRY, a soldier of Colonel Bayley's Regiment, 22 February 1648. [HMC.Ormonde.ii.69]

YOUNG, JOHN, a merchant in Belfast, will refers to his wife Mary, their children Alexander, Hugh, Jane wife of Gilbert McTeer, Charles, Robert, James, and Abigail wife of Robert Milliken and their son William Milliken, Daniel Mussenden in Belfast, William Stevenson in Ballymacarrett; witnesses James Park, Thomas Stevenson and James McTeer all merchants in Belfast, also Thomas Sturgeon in Belfast, probate 4 June 1724. [DRD]

YOUNG, ROBERT, agent of Sir James Cunningham, residing in the Precinct of Portlogh, 1611. [Carew Mss.58]

YOUNG, WILLIAM a gentleman in Ballibun, parish of Donoghmore, Barony of Raphoe, County Donegal, 1659. [C]

YOUNG, WILLIAM, a tenant in Bangor town, County Down, in 1681. [HM]

INDEX TO PEOPLE MENTIONED IN TEXT

Barry, William, 60

Bedlow, Patrick, 7

Bell, Andrew, 9

Bell, John, 9

Bermingham, Edward, 90

Beton, Dick, 47

Black, Samuel, 62

Blackwood, Ann, 10

Blair, Catherine, 11

Blair, Jane, 11

Blair, Mary, 11

Blair, Thomas, 119

Bowden, James, 31, 81

Boyd, Andrew, 11

Boyd, David, 13

Boyd, Elizabeth, 12

Boyd, James, 12, 31

Boyd, Jane, 12

Boyd, Jean, 12

Boyd, Richard, 31

Boyd, Thomas, 12, 93

Buckley, Henry, 6, 90

Burden, Agnes, 11

Burgh, Thomas, 25

Burne, William, 54

Bustard, Robert, 59

Byrne, Daniel, 83

Cadow, John, 63

Calderwood, Andrew, 90

Calderwood, Anna, 90

Caldwell, Joseph, 32

Camak, John, 95

Campbell, Agnes, 16

Campbell, Alexander, 93

Campbell, Alice, 18

Campbell, Catherine, 18

Campbell, Charles, 62, 83, 96

Campbell, Colin, 107

Campbell, David, 17

Campbell, George, 16, 33

Campbell, Jane, 18

Claxton, John, 5

Clement, Hugh, 83

Clerk, Robert, 21

Cobham, James, 76

Cochrane, David, 4

Cochrane, James, 7

Collins, James, 90

Colquhoun, Humphry, 99

Colville, William, 103

Connell, John, 54

Conolly, William, 90

Conyngham, Ann, 62

Conyngham, Archibald, 7

Conyngham, William, 59

Cord, Elizabeth, 55

Corry, John, 83

Cowan, John, 7

Cowan, William, 7

Cowper, Alice, 84

Cowper, James, 84

Crafford, Andrew, 76

Crafford, Anne, 23

Crafford, David, 23

Crafford, Hellenor, 23

Crafford, Janet, 23

Crafford, John, 102

Crafford, Wiliam, 23

Craig, Archibald, 68

Craig, James, 12

Craig, Jane, 29

Craig, John, 24

Crawford, James, 12, 101

Creery, John, 32

Creichton, Andrew, 25

Creichton, David, 25

Creichton, John, 24

Creichton, Robert, 24

Creichton, Mary, 25

Creighton, James, 1

Crenar, Charles, 25

Fullerton, Robert, 36

Fullerton, William, 36

Futon, John, 19

Galland, Benjamin, 119

Gilchrist, Barbara, 80

Gill, John, 81

Gillespie, Elizabeth, 102

Gillespie, Hugh, 45, 102

Godfrey, William, 119

Gordon, Robert, 95

Gore, Ralph, 25, 59

Gorell, Henry, 59

Gowdy, John, 76

Graham, Margaret, 55

Grant, James, 81

Graves, Joseph, 90

Gray, David, 53

Green, Brockill, 83

Greer, Hugh, 70

Greer, Joseph, 100

Gregg, John, 105

Gregson, John, 83

Haddock, John, 23

Haddock, Roger, 23

Hamil, Hugh, 119

Hamilton, Abraham, 25, 59

Hamilton, Alexander, 43

Hamilton, Andrew, 45, 59

Hamilton, Ann, 76

Hamilton, Archibald, 59, 76

Hamilton, Arthur, 51, 76

Hamilton, Charles, 19

Hamilton, Christopher, 59

Hamilton, Claud, 45

Hamilton, Edward, 45

Hamilton, Elizabeth, 42

Hamilton, Gavin, 43

Hamilton, George, 59, 119

Hamilton, Gilbert, 114

Hamilton, James, 25, 42, 47, 58, 76

Hutcheson, Robert, 53

Inglis, David, 53

Inglis, Thomas, 84

Innes, Gilbert, 53

Innes, Joseph, 68

Iredell, Francis, 102

Irvin, Christopher, 81

Irvin, Dorcas, 81

Irvin, James, 81

Irving, Christopher, 54

Irving, Thomas, 54

Jackson, Gilbert, 55

Jackson, James, 55

Jackson, Joan, 119

Jackson, John, 55

Jackson, Thomas, 55

Jameson, Alexander, 7

Jameson, John, 23

Johnston, Baptist, 81

Johnston, George, 111

Leslie, Robert, 62

Lindsay, Bernard, 22

Lindsay, John, 63

Lindsay, Margaret, 63

Lindsay, Robert, 22

Lindsay, Susanna, 63

Linn, Janet, 11

Livingstone, William, 31

Lockhart, John, 13

Loftus, Lettice, 90

Logan, Edward, 105

Long, George, 76

Love, Joseph, 54

Lowry, Robert, 62

Luke, George, 63

Lyons, Colley, 90

McAlexander, Margaret, 72

McArthur, Dennis, 65

McArthur, Elizabeth, 65

McCamrick, John, 79

Maxwell, Jane, 76

Maxwell, John, 76

Maxwell, Patrick, 76

Maxwell, Richard, 76

Meares, James, 53

Mearns, John, 78

Mearns, Thomas, 78

Meredith, Jane, 83

Meredith, John, 83

Milliken, Robert, 120

Milliken, William, 120

Mills, James, 90

Milnatallie, Neil Boy, 1

Mitchell, Elisabeth, 79

Mitchell, Hugh, 79

Mitchell, James, 79

Mitchell, John, 79, 111

Mitchell, Mary, 18

Mitchell, Rose, 79

Mitchell, William, 79

Nesbitt, Albert, 88

Nesbitt, Alexander, 59, 81, 83, 90

Nesbitt, Alice, 90

Nesbitt, Ann, 90

Nesbitt, Catherine, 90

Nesbitt, Duke, 90

Nesbitt, Elizabeth, 90

Nesbitt, Frances, 90

Nesbitt, George, 90

Nesbitt, Gifford, 90

Nesbitt, James, 90

Nesbitt, Jane, 90

Nesbitt, Lettice, 90

Nesbitt, Margaret, 90

Nesbitt, Alexander, 90

Nesbitt, Thomasina, 90

Nesbitt, William, 90

Nicolson, Hugh, 92

Nugent, Oliver, 59

O'Hara, Henry, 46

155

CPSIA information can be obtained
at www.ICGtesting.com
Printed in the USA
FSHW021900130421
80300FS